INTERNATIONAL DEVELOPMENT IN FOCUS

The Rail Freight Challenge for Emerging Economies

How to Regain Modal Share

Bernard Aritua

WORLD BANK GROUP

Contents

Boxes

Figures

Photographs

Foreword

Globally, policy makers and the public aspire for more freight to be moved by rail and waterways. The environmental and societal benefits of such a shift are compelling. Reducing the negative externalities associated with road-based freight, such as truck-induced congestion and noise pollution, is a strong incentive for modal shift from road to rail.

Understanding how to influence modal shift is important because, after several years of relatively low public investment in railways, many emerging economies are making considerable investments in rail infrastructure. One reason for these investments is alignment with commitments to reduce greenhouse gas emissions by moving more freight on low-carbon modes such as railways and inland waterways. Therefore, public policy makers are interested in accelerating modal shift. At the level of firms and industrial sectors, many shippers are also increasingly responding to public sentiment to reduce the negative effects of road-related logistics, further underlining the need for modal shift.

In addition to the environmental and societal drivers, there are macroeconomic reasons for rebalancing modal share in many countries. Policy makers are increasingly concerned about the national logistics costs of road-only freight and the knock-on effect on sectors of the economy for which logistics cost is a key factor. Macro-level indicators such as the Logistics Performance Index and Doing Business, both published by the World Bank; the Global Competitiveness Index, published by the World Economic Forum; and the Global Connectedness Index, produced by DHL, all signal to policy makers the status of national logistics. Several emerging economies have either regressed or remained stagnant on these macro-level indicators. There is therefore a thirst for new ideas and keen interest in practical solutions on how to reduce national logistics costs, many of which require greater use of rail freight transportation. This report contributes to closing this gap.

The report highlights the fact that, in a world of changing global supply chains and logistics, the approach to regaining modal share also needs to change. The new face of "one-stop-shop logistics"—in which several modes of transport are involved in a particular supply chain, often for shippers with a global footprint—increasingly demands an integrated logistics package. Such shippers are less willing to separate out or adjust to the needs of rail-centric freight to move freight by rail. In the past, most railway organizations adopted a "build and they shall come" approach modeled on the proposition that lower rail transportation costs would inevitably lead to modal shift; modern railways focus on understanding the logistics of targeted freight and positioning rail transport services as part of an overall logistics system aimed at meeting the needs of customers.

Rail freight organizations in Europe and North America are responding to new trends in logistics by partnering with road haulers, port operators, forwarders, intermodal terminal operators, and third-party logistics companies to provide the seamless service delivery required by changing supply chains. Rail freight organizations in emerging economies have an opportunity to draw lessons from countries whose railways regained modal share and to reinvent themselves within the framework of a total logistics service demanded by today's growth markets and global supply chains.

Guangzhe Chen
Global Director, Transport Global Practice
The World Bank

Acknowledgments

This report is an output of the Transport Global Practice of the World Bank Group. It was prepared by a team led by Bernard Aritua. The team comprised Norbert Wagener, Jan Havenga, Harrie de Leijer, Timon Stasko, Harold Leupold, Zane Simpson, and Esther Woon Chiew. The need for the study arose from engagements with public railway organizations and policy makers in emerging economies who are concerned about the huge investments in railway infrastructure, which in their experience is not always followed by a concomitant shifting of freight to rail, despite the transportation cost and environmental advantages of rail-based transportation.

The team acknowledges the excellent discussions and feedback from various policy makers and officials from public rail organizations. It is grateful to experts from the following organizations for sharing their experience and insights and providing data: Nuremberg Bayernhafen Freight Village, Duisburger Hafen, BNSF Railway, CSX Railways, Norfolk Southern Railway, Union Pacific Railroad, DB Schenker, ProRail, Transnet, DHL Supply Chain, Freightliner UK, Kuehne & Nagel, Network Rail, Oxera Consulting, Wagener & Herbst, STC-NESTRA, Tibbett & Britten, and the University of Stellenbosch.

The authors are grateful for the support provided by Martha Lawrence, Senior Railways Specialist and leader of the Railways Community of Practice at the World Bank, and for the valuable expert advice received from peer reviewers Yin Yin Lam, Luis C. Blancas Mendivil, Moustafa Baher El-Hefnawy, and Mr. Charles Kunaka. Special thanks to Tong Zhu for his contribution to the analysis.

The team is grateful to Vivien Foster, Karla González Carvajal, and Binyam Reja for providing guidance.

The authors also wish to acknowledge various reports that have been referred to in the study and referenced in this report.

About the Author

Bernard Aritua is a Senior Infrastructure Specialist in the Transport Global Practice of the World Bank Group. He has worked in the field of infrastructure development and economic policy for more than twenty years. During this time, he has led and provided technical input on policy analysis, regulation, institutional reform, and technical design of multimodal transport and freight logistics. Prior to joining the World Bank, he worked in both the private and public sectors in the United Kingdom, Germany, Eastern Europe, Africa, the Middle East, and, more recently, India and China. He is a Chartered Engineer with a PhD in civil engineering from the University of Leeds, United Kingdom.

Executive Summary

THE CHALLENGE FACING RAIL TRANSPORT

At the start of the 20th century, most surface freight was moved by rail. Today a fraction of all freight in most countries is transported by rail; road transportation is the preferred mode for most shippers. Public officials and policy makers in emerging economies are grappling with how to regain or reverse the trend of falling rail modal share.

Many reasons are cited for this decline in rail modal share. At the core is that modal share is now determined by decisions of shippers whose priorities are the balance between total logistics costs and customer satisfaction rather than on the transport mode.

The landscape for global logistics has changed considerably during the past 15–20 years. Even in advanced economies, rail freight organizations that have not woken up to the reality that freight transport is only part of a much larger chain have fared badly.

Compared with unimodal transport by road, any combination of multiple modes faces specific challenges. A key challenge is the additional transshipment and pre- and end haulage operations, which often result in higher door-to-door costs and longer lead times compared with direct trucking. This additional handling affects customers' logistics costs, level of service, or both.

However, multimodal transport can be set up to be competitive and attractive to shippers, especially if customer requirements can be met without their recognizing that the transport chain may involve various combinations of road, rail, and inland waterways. For example, if final customers or shippers of containerized freight see a truck at the destination, and the freight arrives on time at a cost comparable to the unimodal transport option and with service flexibility, they do not care how the various modes were combined as part of a multimodal transport service.

Some rail organizations—particularly in Europe and North America—have responded to the changes in supply chains and regained modal share or reversed a trend of falling shares. By drawing on experience across several emerging economies and relatively successful rail organizations in Europe and North America, this report contributes to closing a critical knowledge gap by highlighting avenues to address the rail freight challenge.

PRIMARY AUDIENCE AND SCOPE OF REPORT

The primary audience for this report is policy makers and senior officials in rail organizations in emerging economies who are grappling with the challenge of how to reverse or slow the loss of rail freight modal share in the modal mix in their countries. This report presents examples and lessons in a format intended to stimulate thinking. It is not a toolkit or policy guide to be followed outside the context of structured policy making; the examples and case studies are not panaceas. The contents highlight good examples and lessons that may be used to inform decisions and broaden discussion of options open to policy makers and senior officials in rail organizations in their country contexts.

WHAT RAIL ORGANIZATIONS AND POLICY MAKERS IN EMERGING ECONOMIES CAN DO TO REGAIN FREIGHT MODAL SHARE OR REVERSE FALLING MODAL SHARE TRENDS

Both rail organizations and policy makers can take actions to reverse the declining modal share of rail. Rail organizations may consider the following.

Implement modern management concepts, and make rail a customer-oriented business

Most railways in emerging economies were developed to move bulk cargo—mostly minerals from mines to ports. By the 1950s, up to 90 percent of all freight in Africa, Latin America, and South Asia was carried by rail. According to the Association of American Railroads, in 1930, rail freight accounted for more than 70 percent of intercity ton miles; by 1960, that share had fallen to just under 45 percent and, by 1980, was under 40 percent. This trend of falling modal share was also evident in most railways in Europe, where the share of volume dropped from 40 percent in 1960 to less than 13 percent in 2000.

Most public railways failed to provide services that met their customers' needs. As a result, many traditional rail customers shifted to road transportation, and new customers did not opt for rail, even for bulky freight transported over long distances. In this vicious circle of falling freight volumes, railways around the world evolved into inefficient, overstaffed, and underfinanced public agencies that no longer had captive markets and faced stiff competition from road transportation.

Lack of funding resulted in wear on rail infrastructure, with little to no maintenance or improvements, and inward-facing rather than customer-oriented organizations. Also, because most funding came from the public sector, railways were generally subject to suffocating regulations on price and service. Moreover, in most emerging economies, priority was given to passenger over freight rail, reinforcing the decline.

To reverse this trend, successful railways have benefitted from institutional and regulatory reforms that enabled service and tariff flexibility to meet customers' demands. Railways in the United States and Germany approached the problem differently, but both focused on customer orientation, with decisions guided by factors such as customer willingness to pay, commodity type and logistics characteristics, and volumes. Customer orientation should be a priority for any railway that aspires to regain modal share.

Focus on core offerings of rail, with specialization and standardization for seamless logistics

Successful railways invest in innovative logistics solutions and infrastructure that play to the strengths of railways while enabling the rail–road interchange. Attempts to regain rail modal share in many countries have targeted multiple opportunities at the same time. As a result, many railways have not built on the inherent competitive advantage of rail to carry bulk products over long distances at relatively low prices, instead targeting market segments for which trucking is much more efficient, provides better risk management for customers, and is more competitively priced. Moreover, in markets where rail has the advantage, investments have not gone to equipment or infrastructure that is vital to bundle cargo, consolidate logistics activities of major customers, and facilitate efficient shuttle services. As demonstrated by numerous case studies in this report, providing opportunities that play to the strengths of rail transportation is an important factor in effecting modal shift.

Develop a strategy for one-stop-shop logistics through full-service packages or collaboration with nontraditional partners

In the face of changed logistics in which rail is only part of a chain and shippers are less concerned about mode, rail organizations need to recognize that total intermodal services are delivered by an ecosystem of public and private entities rather than a single dominant entity. Within this ecosystem, the logistics chain is only as strong as its weakest link, so rail services must seamlessly slot into such chains. Doing so requires an end-to-end view of the total logistics chain and keen understanding of where rail services fit. In the United States, large rail companies that enjoy economies of scale have either become providers of full logistics services or customers of companies that assemble the total package. In Europe, rail organizations have developed strategic partnerships with trucking companies and contract logistics providers and adjusted their service offerings to facilitate the logistics chain. Progressive rail organizations should be open to intermediation by established logistics service providers that can consolidate freight, manage terminals, and allow rail to concentrate on the core rail offering. Some of these intermediary companies invest in physical assets, such as intermodal terminals; are part of wider investments in freight villages; or have software assets and industry knowledge.

Develop a detailed understanding of logistics chains and cost drivers for core customers

Reorientation of railways requires an outward rather than an inward view of freight markets. Most rail strategies focus on internal efficiency, based on the proposition that being competitive and offering high-quality rail service with reliable infrastructure and services are sufficient to regain customer confidence. However, after several decades of poor service, experience shows that being competitive and offering high-quality service are important prerequisites, but not always sufficient, to regaining significant modal share. In a world of modern logistics, railway organizations need to focus more on understanding the needs of specific customers for whom rail delivers a competitive advantage and offer a range and quality of services that fit specific customer needs. Doing so requires investing in research and tailoring strategies to specific customers. Disaggregated data and analysis specific to commodity, supply chain, and logistics drivers may be used to:

- Segment the transport market into natural flow "categories," such as bulk export, mineral exports, domestic minerals, industrial siding-to-siding business, and high-value intermodal (domestic and international) fast-moving consumer goods flows.
- Determine what the natural rail competitive spaces are for each of these flow categories.
- Define what is needed to compete in each category; for example, the logistics requirements for low-cost heavy haul minerals from mines to ports differ significantly from the requirements of wholesale customers of fast-moving consumer goods, which require significant consolidation and bundling.

This evidence can also be used to support the business case with mineral owners, shippers, logistics service providers, and infrastructure providers and to allow central planners to design and invest in railway systems that can be inserted in the logistics chains of customers.

Be alert to trends shaping national and global logistics

The trends toward containerization and reorientation of supply chains disrupted national and global logistics in the 20th century. Several rail organizations failed to respond in time and lost modal share as a result. Trends shaping current logistics include new trade routes; new logistics concepts (such as cross-chain control and synchromodality); and disruptive technologies such as blockchain, big data analytics, advanced robotics, and artificial intelligence, which are reshaping end-to-end logistics and will inevitably affect the role of carriers and the decisions of shippers. Modern railways are keeping up and experimenting with various partners on the logistics implications.

In many countries the role of public and private rail organizations that are responsible for infrastructure and operations can be distinguished from that of policy makers and regulators. Policy makers have a range of instruments at their disposal beyond investments in infrastructure that can be used to influence modal choice. Policy makers at various levels of local and central governments can use a combination of policy instruments to overcome barriers, address market failures, and create opportunities for increased use of rail freight. The case studies in this report show that the following actions can have an impact.

Support institutional and regulatory reforms that enable inefficient and monopolistic state railways to transition toward market-oriented enterprises that are responsive to customers

Rail organizations that have set out on the path of reform require strong and sustained support to implement change. In the United States, such support came in the form of deregulation, which allowed flexibility in price and service. Deregulation also enabled and provided incentives for railroad companies to invest in infrastructure and to divest from routes and services that were not viable. In Europe, not all reforms resulted in increased modal share. For instance, in the United Kingdom, reforms resulted in significant loss of rail market share. Nevertheless, the companies that emerged now offer rail services that are responsive to their customers. In Germany and the Netherlands, reforms resulted in stronger rail organizations and greater use of rail freight transportation.

Use spatial planning and land use measures to encourage clustering of logistics activities close to railways

Rail freight transportation is especially competitive when cargo can be consolidated and flows matched to reach critical volumes over relatively long distances. Therefore, policy makers and governments can use long-term planning, zoning regulations, and permits to promote private investment and public–private partnerships in ways that allow for densification of volumes and services that are suited to rail logistics. Creation of logistics zones on the outskirts of cities can be used to combine warehousing and truck parking facilities; freight villages can be developed to enable shippers and logistics providers to settle in organized estates with multimodal options built into the design through regulation. In Europe, zoning regulations prohibit establishment of logistics facilities without two or more transport modes: every logistics cluster or freight village must have road and rail or inland waterway connections embedded in the planning. This is not the case in many emerging economies, where logistics facilities often have only a road connection and rail connectivity is an afterthought rather than integrated into planning and design.

Invest in detailed and disaggregated analysis of national freight flows to inform decisions about where to target interventions or public investment to ensure that the right freight flows on the right mode and maximizes efficient use of the entire transport and logistics network

Most emerging economies do not have the advantage of several decades of gradual development of national or regional logistics. Policy makers thus have limited evidence on commodity volumes, freight types, transport supply, origins and destinations of freight, and key actors in supply chains. If such evidence exists, it is often incomplete or partial. In most cases, for example, data on road traffic counts are not related to industry productivity data, warehousing, or rail data and vice versa, making it difficult to make informed policy decisions about where to target interventions or public investment. To address this shortfall, policy makers need to invest in a detailed understanding of freight flows across geography and industry supply chains. For example, in South Africa, the public port–rail company uses a disaggregated freight flow model developed in collaboration with a research institute to analyze scenarios and conduct long-term planning. The disaggregated freight flows provide insight into various sectors and enable development of specific solutions based on granular evidence. Such an approach, modeled on experience from Germany, Norway, and Sweden, can be used to better understand the status of national freight and give a clear view of the implications of efforts to improve rail-centric logistics.

Use taxes, subsidies, and incentives to create momentum for multimodal transport

Direct and indirect interventions through taxes, incentives, and subsidies can affect the attractiveness of one transport mode, or route, over another. Strategically selected pilots and simulations can demonstrate innovations in logistics that result in freight being bundled in ways that are suited to transport services in which rail transportation plays a key role. The benefits to society and the environment often justify the simulations and pilots that promote multimodal transport. Once momentum is created, shippers may be inclined to adopt rail-based solutions.

Abbreviations

2PL	second-party logistics
3PL	third-party logistics
4C	cross-chain control center
4PL	fourth-party logistics
BNSFL	BNSF Logistics
CAA	Autonomous Community of Aragón
EU	European Union
FFC	First Freight Co. (Russian Federation)
FV	freight village
GDP	gross domestic product
IMC	intermodal marketing company
IT	information technology
LPI	Logistics Performance Index
LSP	logistics service provider
RZD	Russian Railways

1 Rail Freight in Emerging Economies

Efficient freight transportation is critical to economic development. The availability of transport infrastructure and services affects national and global development patterns and can be a boost or barrier to economic growth. Transportation infrastructure and logistics investments link factors of production in a web of relationships between producers and consumers and everything in between. In this sense, the transportation and logistics network is the backbone of any economy.

RAIL FREIGHT AND ECONOMIC DEVELOPMENT IN EMERGING ECONOMIES

Rail freight is important to economic development because of its comparative economic advantages in serving certain forms and flows of freight. Countries with well-functioning freight railways are more competitive and reap wider benefits of balanced transport systems in which the right freight moves on the right mode (World Bank 2009).

The economic benefits of freight transport accrue when it allows producers from developing countries to affordably access inputs of raw materials, intermediate goods, and other resources and to consign their final products to markets. Well-run railways provide the capacity and services required by heavy industry, thus facilitating trade, economic specialization, and economic growth.

In some regions of Central Asia, Eastern Europe, South Asia, Southeast Asia, and Sub-Saharan Africa characterized by groupings of many small countries, rail freight can increase economic integration by providing access to international and regional markets and connecting landlocked countries. Freight railways also deliver benefits that are increasingly valued by policy makers, particularly in the areas of safety and the environment. As a result, countries increasingly include freight rail on the critical path to decarbonizing and achieving commitments toward sustainable development. Many emerging economies identified modal shift from road to rail and inland waterways as a major part of their strategy to reduce greenhouse emissions under their Nationally Determined Contribution commitments.

Sustainable transport policies should enhance the role and scale of rail freight transport. On the one hand, policy makers in developing countries may be reluctant to support greater use of railways if doing so means that their industries endure poor freight transport services that add to their logistics costs. On the other hand, well-managed freight railways are needed to contribute to economic development, and the long-term benefits are potentially significant.

The budgetary impact of rail freight transport is also an important consideration for policy makers. Freight railways that are poorly conceived—without a clear path for getting freight onto rail—or poorly managed and maintained are a drain on national budgets, resulting in misallocation of scarce resources that could be used more productively in other sectors. Such railways invariably have a large negative budgetary impact.

Macro-level indicators often reveal the need for improvement in national logistics and the potential of railways. The Logistics Performance Index, published by the World Bank every two years, reflects perceptions of a country's logistics or the ease with which goods and services can be moved as and when they are needed or desired by customers. It is based on the results of a questionnaire administered in 160 countries. Many policy makers are keen to achieve high rankings.

Logistics performance and economic performance are correlated: Countries that score high on the Logistics Performance Index also have higher income per capita, as figure 1.1 shows. Improvement in logistics—including the critical role of railways—is therefore an important development issue.

Other macro-level indexes also have implications for policy makers. The Global Competitiveness Index, published by the World Economic Forum,

FIGURE 1.1

Correlation between per capita GDP and LPI score, 2018

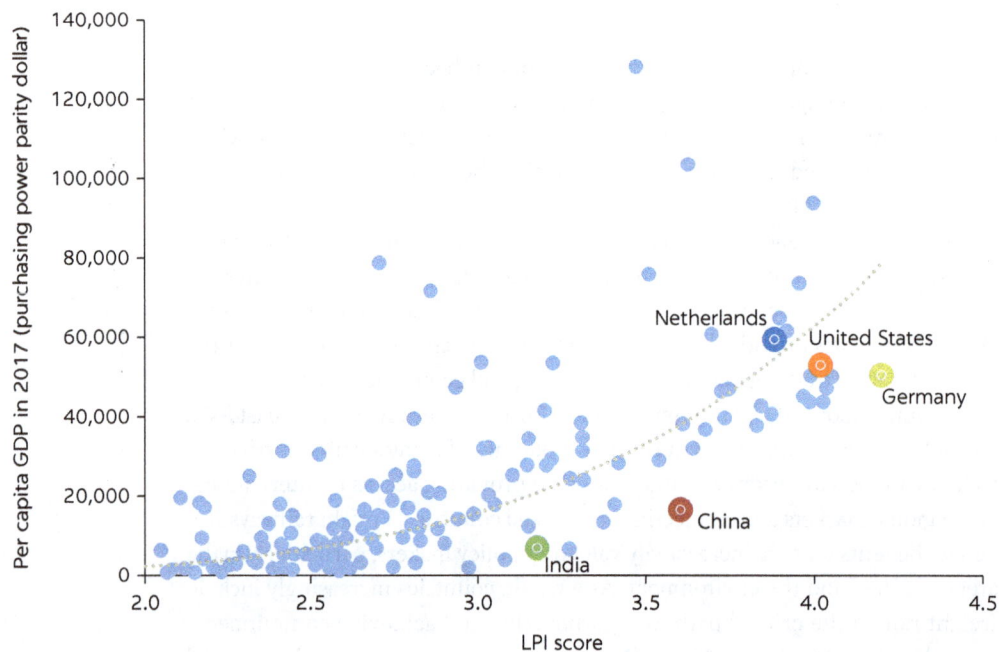

Source: World Bank 2018.
Note: LPI scores range from 1 (lowest) to 5 (highest). GDP = gross domestic product; LPI = Logistics Performance Index.

seeks to capture the combination of factors believed to make countries competitive. It defines competitiveness as the set of institutions, policies, and factors that determine a country's level of productivity, which sets the level of prosperity an economy can achieve. The ease with which freight is moved often plays a crucial role in the rankings.

Other indicators include the Global Connectedness Index, produced by DHL, which maps the relationship between the flow of trade, capital, information, and people. It measures the depth of domestic activity, geographic distribution, and in–out flows.

These macro indicators signal to policy makers the status of national logistics. The question for them, especially in emerging economies, is where to focus limited resources and policy instruments.

Figure 1.2 shows the correlation between the positions of countries on the macro indexes and the maturity of their logistics. Unsurprisingly, countries in Europe and North America that have well-developed rail freight also perform better on the macro logistics indicators. Macro indicators alert policy makers to difficulties with national logistics.

There is a clear inverse relationship between logistics costs as a percentage of gross domestic product (GDP) and third-party logistics revenues. Outsourcing logistics services to specialist providers benefits firms and reduces logistics costs through economies of scale, with railways playing an important role.

FIGURE 1.2

Performance of logistics in selected countries, 2018

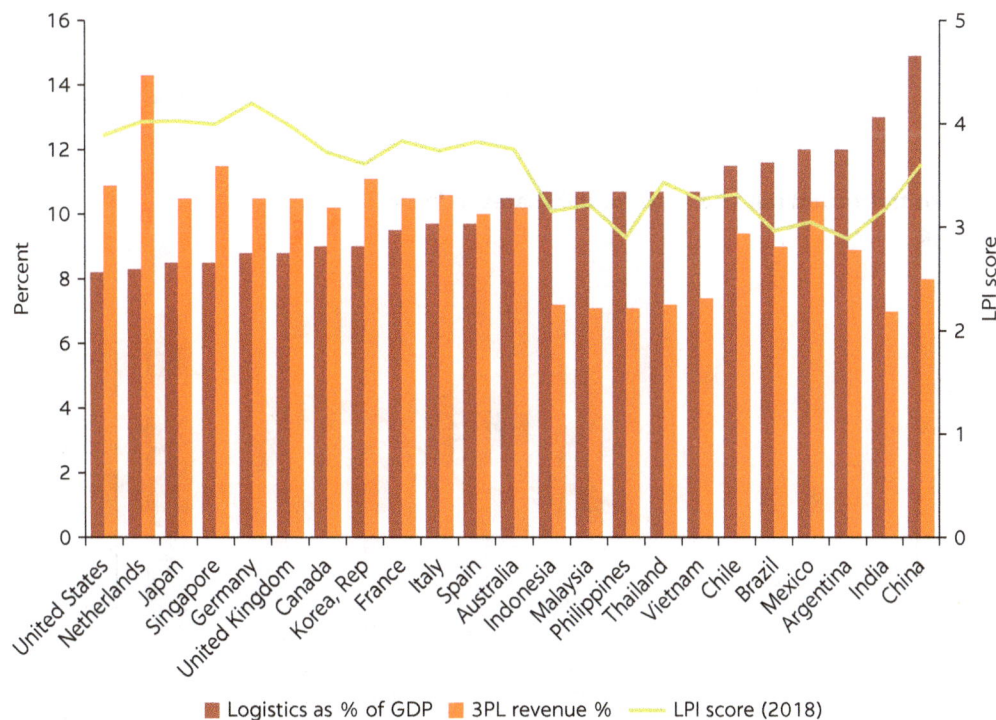

Source: Data from the World Bank Group and Armstrong & Associates, Inc.
Note: 3PL = third-party logistics; GDP = gross domestic product; LPI = Logistics Performance Index.

INCREASING INVESTMENT IN RAILWAYS AND EFFORTS TO REVERSE THE LOSS OF MODAL SHARE

Nearly half of the world's functional rail network is in emerging economies, but the share of freight carried by rail in these countries is much smaller than it used to be. In some countries, the modal share represents a small percentage of growing national freight volume.

In 1950, up to 90 percent of all freight in Africa, Latin America, and South Asia was carried by rail. In much of the emerging world, the growth of railways was driven by the need to move bulk minerals from mines to ports in the colonial era. The fortunes of railways changed sharply with the rise of road transportation in the mid-20th century, as postcolonial independent countries invested heavily in road infrastructure, creating extensive highway networks. The capabilities of road vehicles and the quality of the infrastructure improved rapidly, and rail struggled to keep up. The nascent air transportation industry did not compete for much of the freight traveling on rail, but it presented an alternative for shipping of high-value goods.

Although consistent data series going back to the mid-1900s are not available, the decline in rail's freight modal share is widely acknowledged and confirmed by several sources. For example, figure 1.3 shows the situation in India. Driven mostly by private consumption, India is one of the world's fastest-growing emerging economies, with average GDP growth rate exceeding 7 percent for most of the past two decades. The total volume of freight has soared, but the volume of freight carried by rail has fallen consistently. India has embarked on an ambitious program of investment and interventions to reverse the trend.

Economic growth in emerging economies creates potential demand for rail logistics. But the lack of customer orientation of most railways limits the attractiveness of rail for most shippers. Despite economic geography features and demand for rail services from the increased volumes of manufactured goods and raw materials, the volume of freight moved by rail has fallen short of the GDP growth registered in most countries. Several years of sustainable growth in

FIGURE 1.3

Freight traffic and rail and road modal shares in India, 1950–2015

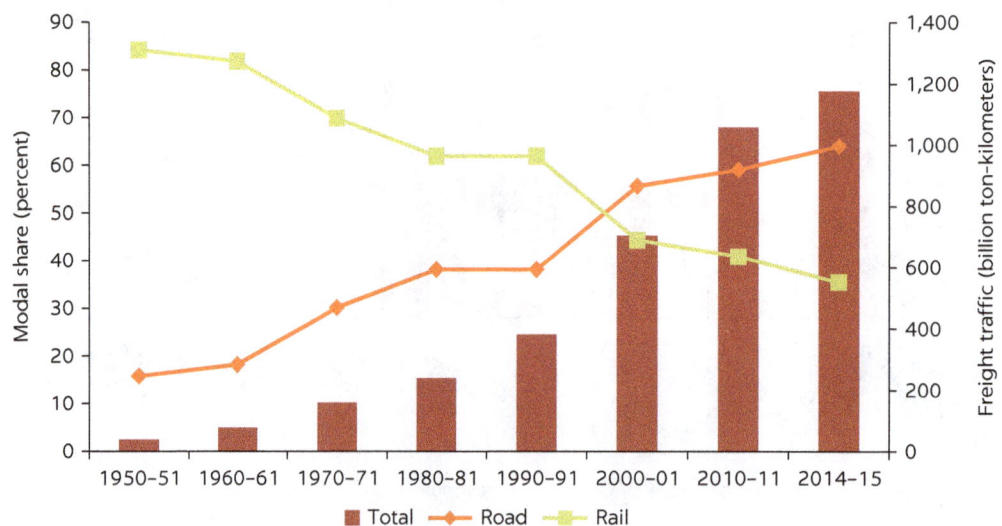

Source: Indian Railways.

Latin America led to growth in the trucking sector, at a time when rail modal share fell across the continent, a decline attributed to a lack of investment in rail infrastructure and inefficiencies in publicly held rail corporations. Box 1.1 captures the experience of rail reforms in Mexico.

The experience in Asian countries has been mixed. In general, freight rail modal share has fallen, even though absolute national freight volumes have risen in some countries. In Central Asia, the collapse of the Soviet Union created major challenges for the former republics—the newly independent countries no longer had a central planning system, and controlling traffic between countries at the new national borders proved difficult. Other countries in Asia also have problems with their railway systems. In the Philippines, operating services have declined, partly because of deteriorating infrastructure and lack of maintenance, and an improved highway system has given trucks a competitive advantage over rail. In many Southeast Asian countries, railways carry only a small proportion of final tonnage. In Malaysia, for example, rail carries only about 5 percent of total freight tonnage, according to the Asian Development Bank (2017).

Africa has seen a resurgence of plans to build new standard-gauge lines to revive the freight rail sector (see the example of Ethiopia in box 1.2). The railway lines on the continent were originally built by the European colonial powers to export bulk products. After independence, these networks were broken up by

---

BOX 1.1

Turning around rail freight in Mexico

In the 1980s, Mexico's railways were suffering from poor productivity, significant operating deficits, and dwindling freight volumes. After unsuccessful attempts to overhaul the vertically integrated national railway company, the Mexican government instituted reforms to open the railway sector to private investment and operation.

Between 1996 and 1999, three major concessions were awarded that guaranteed 30-year exclusive operating rights under 50-year operation and maintenance contracts. The concessions were allocated by geographic region and were designed to spark competition through alternative access to key markets, parallel routings, and use of trackage rights along specified segments of the network.

The results of the reform have been good. Freight tariffs have dropped, government subsidies for freight services have been eliminated, and productivity has risen dramatically. Implementing the competitive track access rights, however, has been a challenge. In 2016, a dedicated railway regulator was established to address track access and tariff disputes, among other issues.

Source: World Bank 2017.

BOX 1.2

Addis Ababa–Djibouti standard-gauge railway

A 750-kilometer standard-gauge railway linking Ethiopia's capital Addis Ababa with Djibouti and its port of Doraleh has been built at a cost of approximately $4.5 billion. With financing from the China Exim Bank, operations were inaugurated in January 2018. The railway line has a capacity of 25 million tons per year. The new line runs roughly parallel to an old meter-gauge Ethio–Djibouti Railway for most of its length.

Source: Ethiopian Railway Corp.

the new national borders, leading to reductions in market size and economies of scale (African Development Bank 2015). In many African countries, railways came under the jurisdiction of the public sector, which resulted in inefficient, overstaffed, and underfinanced railway organizations that were not able to provide good service and fell short on maintenance (exceptions are South Africa and some North African countries). In addition, as in some countries elsewhere, priority in financing and policy was given to road transportation. Road transport in Africa has not faced the same regulations and control as railway industries, leading to unfair competition between road and rail. In addition, the lack of financing and expertise has resulted in extreme wear on the existing rail infrastructure and little to no maintenance or improvements. Many African countries began to receive financing through the World Bank and other donors in the mid-1990s, with a drive toward public–private partnerships, but few partnerships have resulted in substantial growth in the modal share of rail.

The challenge for these new and planned investments in standard-gauge railways is where the freight will come from. Without addressing this fundamental issue, emerging countries run the risk of investing in stranded assets, and the railways could potentially suffer the same fate as their predecessors.

One of the major challenges of railways in emerging economies is the inability to exploit rail economics to the same extent as was possible in Canada and the United States. In the four decades since 1980, the total route-kilometer network of the North American rail systems declined by about 40 percent. At the same time, the combined Chinese, Indian, and Russian Federation network grew by about 10 percent. But both systems doubled output (in ton-kilometers), indicating higher returns to density in North America.

There are also major differences in other productivity measures, such as employees per route-kilometer and ton-kilometers per employee output, between railway systems in North America and most emerging economies. Railways in emerging economies tend to rely on large volumes of "captured" traffic, such as low-value minerals, whereas North American railways were "forced" to deal with the switch to high-value traffic, the logistics of which are more challenging. Circumstances in the United States forced railroad companies to deal with intermodality and third-party logistics companies, thereby creating opportunities for new markets, which have been stable and lucrative. Many emerging economies have not yet solved this problem.

ACTIONS BY EMERGING ECONOMIES

A challenge for policy makers and rail organizations in emerging economies is how to shift more freight to rail. At a time when there is a strong case for investment in the rail sector, many decision makers are keen to draw lessons from other relatively successful countries. Several emerging economies are either making significant investments aimed at reviving their railway sectors or designing master plans that prioritize freight rail infrastructure. Among emerging economies, China has experienced the most rapid rail network expansion, growing from 22,000 kilometers of poorly maintained and war-damaged railway tracks in 1949 to 121,000 kilometers in 2015 (box 1.3). In mid-2016, the government of China revised its target to 175,000 kilometers by 2025. Much of the focus of this expansion has been on passenger rail, however. Despite breathtaking growth in national freight volumes since 1998, the share of freight moved by railways in China dropped from 22 percent in 2008 to 16 percent in 2016. Over the

BOX 1.3

Maintaining centralized control of rail in China

Railway reform in China differs from reform in most countries. The government of China has stuck to a centralized administration and made a publicly financed network expansion program its priority.

China has yet to fully embrace many of the options promoted by the World Bank, such as opening the sector to private sector participants and investors, allowing freight tariffs to be market-determined, and making a clear separation between regulatory and commercial functions.

In 2013, the Ministry of Railways was dissolved, and policy and regulatory functions were separated from

commercial functions. However, unlike in other countries, the functions are still wholly under the public sector. The rail sector's functions are administered by three public entities. The Ministry of Transportation is responsible for overall transport sector planning and development policy; the State Railways Administration, a new body under the Ministry of Transportation, is responsible for setting technical standards, setting and overseeing safety standards, and monitoring the quality of transport service and construction; and the China Railway Corporation, a state-owned enterprise, is responsible for commercial operation of the railways.

Source: World Bank 2017.

BOX 1.4

Stabilizing the freight rail sector in the Russian Federation

After the dissolution of the Soviet Union, the Russian railway industry entered challenging times. Freight volumes declined, financial losses mounted, assets deteriorated, and operational productivity declined. The government embarked on an ambitious railway reform program, which achieved impressive results. Between 1995 and 2009, freight turnover rose 87 percent before succumbing to the effects of the 2008 global economic crisis. Since 2010, freight turnover has been steadily increasing.

As part of the reform, the Ministry of Railways was separated into the Federal Railway Transport Agency as regulator and Russian Railways (RZD), a state-owned company in charge of railway infrastructure and train operations for freight and passengers. In 2003, RZD was reconstituted as a joint stockholding company. RZD then created 63 subsidiary companies focusing on niche markets.

By 2005, one-third of the country's freight moved in privately owned wagons; by 2013, private operators owned 80 percent of the wagon fleet. In 2011, Independent Transport Co. paid Rub 125.5 billion ($4.3 billion) for 75 percent ownership of First Freight Co. (FFC), which owned roughly half of RZD's freight wagons. It bought the remaining 25 percent of the shares in 2012 for Rub 50 billion ($1.6 billion).

As part of the focus on creating competition, RZD capitalized FFC with 200,000 wagons and created Second Freight Co., which it capitalized with 217,000 wagons. Both companies faced competition from independent operators set up by major natural resources companies. In 2012, RZD completed the sale of its shares in FFC and transferred a substantial portion of its wagon inventory to its subsidiaries.

Source: World Bank 2017.

same period, the share of freight activity by highways and waterways increased. Nearly all market share lost by rail shifted to highways and inland waterways (World Bank 2017).

After the dissolution of the Soviet Union, rail freight volumes in Russia declined to less than 10 percent of total national freight. The Russian government embarked on an ambitious railway reform and investment program, which has stabilized the sector (box 1.4).

India also invested heavily in freight rail infrastructure, including 3,400 kilometers of exclusive freight-only lines (the Eastern & Western Dedicated Freight Corridors), which will eventually form a core Golden Quadrilateral of freight-only railways connecting the major cities of New Delhi, Kolkata, Chennai, and Mumbai.

In addition to investing in core track and signaling infrastructure, many countries are also considering investments in information management, rolling stock, and logistics facilities. What is evident from actions and policy statements is that revival of freight rail is considered a critical element of development. The issue is how to reconfigure the role of railways. The next chapter discusses trends that have a bearing on options.

REFERENCES

African Development Bank. 2015. *Rail Infrastructure in Africa: Financing Policy Options.* Abidjan: African Development Bank.

Armstrong & Associates, Inc. https://www.3plogistics.com.

Asian Development Bank. 2017. *Unlocking the Potential of Railways: A Railway Strategy for CAREC, 2017–2030.* Central Asia Regional Economic Cooperation Program. Manila: Asian Development Bank.

Indian Railways. 2016. *Indian Railways Statistical Year Book India 2016.* New Delhi: Indian Railways.

World Bank. 2009. *Freight Transport for Development Toolkit: Rail Freight.* Washington DC: World Bank.

World Bank. 2017. *Railway Reform: Toolkit for Improving Rail Sector Performance.* Washington, DC: World Bank.

2 Global Trends Shaping Transport and Logistics

Transport and logistics underpin many sectors of the economy in all countries. Changes in both have reshaped the way value chains and trade relationships are configured. This chapter highlights the main changes in the past and draws attention to emerging trends.

CONTAINERIZATION AND THE TRANSFORMATION OF GLOBAL FREIGHT TRANSPORT IN THE 20TH CENTURY

Shipping containers, which are essentially metal boxes of standardized dimensions, transformed logistics in the 20th century (Levinson 2008). A century after rail first challenged the dominance of water transport, and at a time when the railroad industry was reeling, adoption of standardized containers by ocean shipping companies created new opportunities to reconfigure logistics (Lowe 2005).

In the 1950s, freight handling and shipping required a great deal of time at ports. The loading and unloading of ships was a time-consuming, expensive, and risky process. A hodgepodge of mixed cargo would be tallied and stored in warehouses before large crews of longshoremen arranged it on pallets. The pallets were then pulled onto the ships by cranes on the ships and unloaded and rearranged in the ships' holds, with minimal automation and mostly strenuous manual labor. Theft was rampant, with antagonistic labor–management relations serving as an excuse. The result was a system that made ocean shipping unappealing. Port operations were expensive, both in time and money, and constituted a large part of overall logistics costs.

The inefficiencies of ship loading and unloading prompted numerous experiments with containerization. Containers could be loaded rapidly by cranes, without the risks or inefficiencies of repacking. Container technology was not standardized, however, which led to new inefficiencies. Not all cranes or trucks could handle all containers. Different size containers did not stack well. There was widespread recognition of the need for a standard, but with multiple vested interests setting one was challenging.

Eventually, the International Standards Organization created a set of standard sizes that was adopted by the logistics industry. With containers standardized, the next modification was design of ships and ports to handle their processing as efficiently as possible. Containerization and related changes, such as ship growth, made ocean shipping far more attractive.

Among the many forces that pushed globalization forward in the 20th century, the improvement in ocean shipping performance was significant. Capital became more mobile as international shipping became reliable. Supply chains grew longer as manufacturing dispersed farther from centers of consumption. As a result, shipping volumes increased, presenting new opportunities for railways (AASHTO 2017).

The natural consolidation of cargo also favored rail economics, especially where rail could capitalize on it. Successful ports featured rail evacuation and entry into the port, dry ports, and extended gates served by rail shuttles as well as large volume contracts between railways, ports, shipping lines, merchants, and logistics service providers. The emergence of new logistics models created opportunities for railways to be inserted into logistics systems and to fully benefit from this consolidation.

As a next step, railways could benefit by transferring all the shipping container advantages to purely domestic movements—using containers to consolidate freight on both sides of domestic freight movements. Doing so requires mature service design, as achieved in the United States, where domestic container growth outstripped international growth for more than a decade and containers account for a large share of the freight market and revenues.

THE RISE OF THIRD-PARTY LOGISTICS AND THE "NEW NORMAL" FOR SUPPLY CHAINS

Containerization, and other improvements in ocean shipping, led to the lengthening of supply chains. Cheaper and better transport allowed corporations to find the cheapest manufacturing locations, without being restricted by distances. The changes to supply chains went beyond simply lengthening them: supply chains became more complex as the number of firms involved increased in an effort to achieve vertical integration.

With more mobile capital, there was also an opportunity to capitalize on economies of scale. As a result, suppliers began to specialize in niches and expand to meet the needs of a global client base. Previously, each vertically integrated firm needed its own local facility for each step of the value chain. With changes in supply chains, several elements could be outsourced to different providers, often located across the globe.

Supply chains became even more sophisticated with the rise of just-in-time and lean manufacturing approaches. Toyota started signing contracts with suppliers to deliver small batches of intermediate products exactly when they were needed, instead of holding large inventories, which tied up capital and increased storage costs. Many U.S. companies sought to imitate Toyota's success, with two-thirds of Fortune 500 companies implementing a variant of the just-in-time approach (Lieb and Bentz 2004).

The main advantage of this approach is lower inventory requirements, as trust is built at multiple levels. Manufacturers have to trust the quality and timeliness of their suppliers. They also have to trust the reliability and timeliness of their logistics providers. For this reason, better shipping has enabled just-in-time growth, which has placed higher demands on the shipping industry. Manufacturers using a just-in-time approach began seeking closer relationships with transport companies, a vital part in the chain for on-time delivery.

Figure 2.1 depicts the transition to the "new normal" for supply chains. Changes in the transportation industry prompted manufacturers and retailers to redesign their operations, fundamentally altering the nature of supply chains. The resulting supply chains were long and complex; exhibited strong economies of scale; and were expected to be fast, reliable, and transparent. This combination of reality and demands was challenging for logistics departments and contributed to the emergence of the third-party logistics (3PL) industry.[1]

The dramatic rise of 3PLs in the United States is commonly attributed to deregulation of the trucking industry, which led to specialization in service provision. The emergence of 3PLs can be viewed as an extension of the way in which the manufacturing industry moved from vertical integration to horizontal integration, with each step benefitting from new economies of scale. The core of the 3PL value proposition is the economies of scale that result from 3PLs' specialization in managing supply chains. In particular, 3PLs are well positioned to invest in tools, knowledge, and people at a level that shippers often would not.

In North America, freight forwarders and the container shipping lines originate much of the flow of international containers on rail. But intermodal marketing companies (IMCs) act as intermediaries between Class 1 rail carriers and asset-based truck carriers, on the one hand, and shippers and other retail customers, on the other. IMCs do not own heavy assets, such as trains or trucks; their assets are information technology (IT), human resources, and occasionally intermodal equipment such as containers and chassis. IMCs add value to shippers by securing blocks of rail linehaul and truck drayage capacity, including at peak periods, at rates or times that retail customers would not be able to access individually. They do so by entering into long-term contracts with rail and truck carriers, which give them access to a wide array of carriers. IMCs form the backbone of successful exploitation of rail economics and are responsible for creating

FIGURE 2.1

Evolution of the "new normal" for supply chains

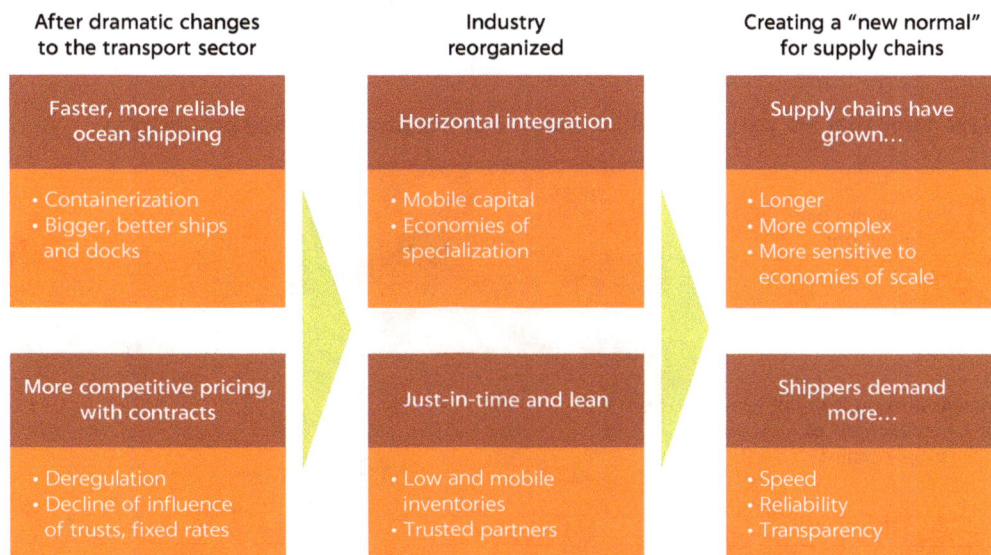

After dramatic changes to the transport sector	Industry reorganized	Creating a "new normal" for supply chains
Faster, more reliable ocean shipping • Containerization • Bigger, better ships and docks	**Horizontal integration** • Mobile capital • Economies of specialization	**Supply chains have grown…** • Longer • More complex • More sensitive to economies of scale
More competitive pricing, with contracts • Deregulation • Decline of influence of trusts, fixed rates	**Just-in-time and lean** • Low and mobile inventories • Trusted partners	**Shippers demand more…** • Speed • Reliability • Transparency

opportunities for rail to enter high-value market segments. A similar path was followed in Europe, with major successes from companies such as Hupac, Kombiverkehr, and others. The experience from Europe and the United States shows that rail organizations need to be willing to wholesale space to intermediaries. Railways in the developing world are not used to doing so, and most of their 3PL industries lack the competency to execute complex logistics. Wholesaling makes it much easier for rail to be inserted into longer and more complex supply chains, because it allows railway organizations to concentrate on mass, long haul, and even intermodal heavy haul. In South Africa, heavy haul to single customers is so efficient that mineral heavy haul costs less than $0.01 per ton-kilometer. Higher-value cargo could also be shipped inexpensively, but the wholesale mind shift remains difficult to make. Figure 2.2 shows additional services that are increasingly part of the value proposition from 3PLs. The challenge for policy makers is to develop a road map that allows the diverse capabilities to be nurtured so that 3PLs offer a broader range of services to suit customer requirements.

Some 3PL providers invest in physical infrastructure, such as warehousing and distribution facilities, and IT platforms. By outsourcing to these providers, shippers avoid the need to tie up capital, as well as the risks associated with infrastructure investment, such as the risk that an expensive automated distribution center will not be needed in two years because of a change in demand. By aggregating multiple types of demand, 3PLs can mitigate some of the risk that shippers would face investing on their own. The same principle applies to seasonality. Shared assets can have higher utilization rates, making them more cost-effective.

In addition to investing in physical infrastructure, such as warehouses, 3PLs invest in tools to facilitate niche services. IT systems are among the most important assets of 3PLs. In a 2017 survey of shippers, 93 percent indicated that IT capabilities were a necessary element of 3PL expertise. Most shippers indicated that 3PLs must have IT tools with execution and transaction-based capabilities for planning and managing transportation and operating distribution centers, as well as web portals for booking and tracking. Tactical and strategic tools can be developed for the benefit of multiple clients, mitigating the risk of investment in much the same way that physical infrastructure, such as a warehouse, does. The use of the same IT tools by multiple clients has added benefits if one client is a supplier of the other, with the 3PL's IT system acting as a bridge. The result is tools that improve traceability, visibility, and reliability, at a lower cost (figure 2.3).

FIGURE 2.2

New items that are part of the third-party logistics provider value proposition

FIGURE 2.3

Investment by third-party logistics providers to help shippers manage the "new normal"

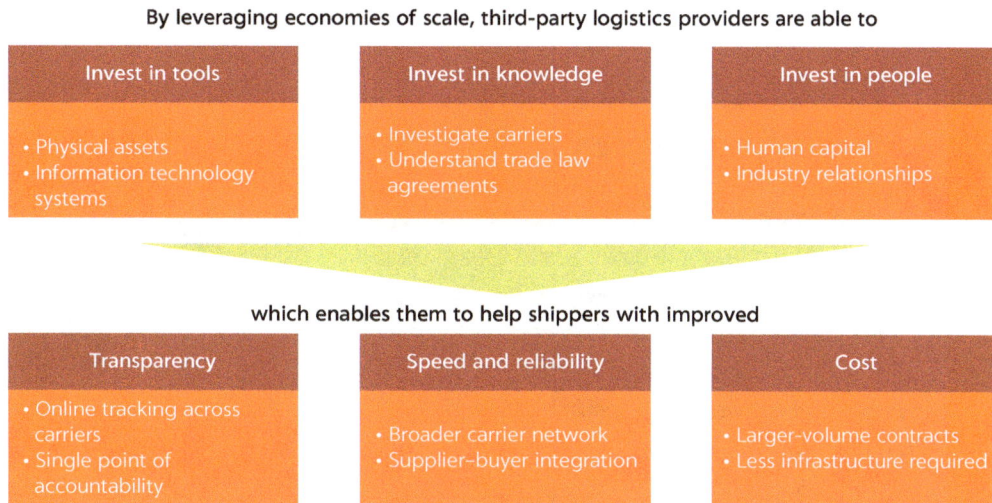

By leveraging economies of scale, third-party logistics providers are able to

Invest in tools	Invest in knowledge	Invest in people
• Physical assets • Information technology systems	• Investigate carriers • Understand trade law agreements	• Human capital • Industry relationships

which enables them to help shippers with improved

Transparency	Speed and reliability	Cost
• Online tracking across carriers • Single point of accountability	• Broader carrier network • Supplier–buyer integration	• Larger-volume contracts • Less infrastructure required

Industry knowledge, although less tangible than the tools 3PLs own, is extremely valuable and often goes beyond the knowledge a shipper's logistics team might acquire on its own. Given the range of clients they serve, 3PLs investigate a large and diverse set of carriers. Brokers have historically checked their carriers' operating authority and insurance, as well as business references. In addition, by working directly for several clients, 3PLs gain a deeper understanding of entire sectors and regions. Large 3PLs regularly work with hundreds of carriers. When a carrier cancels, or a shipper has an emergency shipment, a 3PL with such broad knowledge of carriers has an advantage in finding an alternative, without the need to rush through new background checks. Its knowledge improves reliability for shippers.

3PLs also develop expertise in applicable laws, including complex customs rules and preferential trade agreements, making entry smoother for their clients, who might otherwise need to invest in mastering foreign legal and regulatory systems. The people who work for 3PLs also gain expertise in increasingly sophisticated methodologies for supply chain optimization. It is not cost-effective for a single shipper to keep in-house experts for specialist subjects; several shippers often share a single resource.

3PLs offer specialized services to shippers as part of their value proposition. Shippers report experiencing quantifiable benefits from their use of 3PLs. According to the 2017 *Third-Party Logistics Study* (Capgemini 2018), shippers report both logistics cost savings (9 percent) and inventory cost savings (5 percent) from their use of 3PLs; they report average reductions in fixed logistics costs of 15 percent. Shippers also report increased order fill rates and order accuracy.

The use of 3PL providers is not ubiquitous or without disadvantages. The main disadvantage is that the shipper loses some control over its supply chain. Integration of multiple IT systems can also prove challenging; switching to a 3PL may be accompanied by disruptions that could result in the loss of customers. If the shipper is large and has invested heavily in logistics capabilities, it may already have many of the resources available to 3PLs and may not see as many benefits as smaller counterparts. One of the main reasons shippers cite for not using 3PLs is that logistics is a core competency (Capgemini 2018).

Most shippers outsource operational tasks, but many entrust tech-heavy and strategic logistics services to 3PLs (figure 2.4).

FIGURE 2.4

Share of services that shippers outsource to third-party logistics providers, 2017

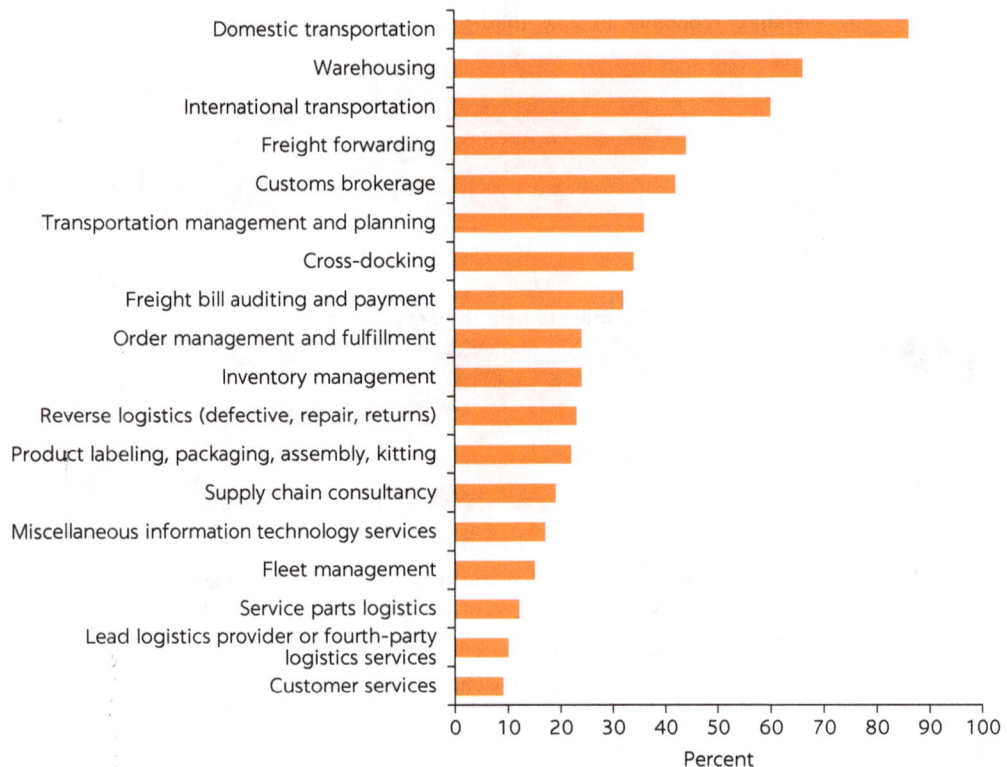

Source: Capgemini 2018.

DISRUPTIVE TECHNOLOGIES TRANSFORMING INDUSTRIAL PRODUCTIVITY AND LOGISTICS IN THE 21ST CENTURY

Globally, many rail organizations did not keep up with the changing trends of containerization and the realignment of supply chains in the 20th century. The impact of these trends on rail organizations has been dramatic; the emergence of 3PLs has added to the pressure on railways to do things differently.

Important changes will shape the way logistics chains are configured in the future. Railway organizations need to be alert to the following trends:

- *New trade routes and rapid urbanization in cities.* Most of the strong recovery after the 2008 global economic crisis and the growth in overall global consumption has been in Asia. Most production will focus on meeting demand in Asia, where the middle class is growing and more than 80 cities are expected to produce more than $100 billion each in gross domestic product by 2030. Railways closer to this center of gravity need to configure services accordingly. Countries in the rest of the world will have opportunities in niche exports, such as food products for megacities. Exporting these products requires specialized intermodal logistics that allow for easy road–rail–maritime transfer and investments in temperature-controlled warehousing; sorting and grading facilities; reefer containers; time-sensitive logistics; and improved checking, inspection, and clearance procedures. New trade routes, such as those associated with the Belt and Road Initiative, create opportunities for trade between China and the rest of the world. Railways are the backbone of several of these corridors.

- *New platforms and advances in technology.* The role of technologies such as blockchain, big data analytics, robotics, and artificial intelligence in end-to-end logistics will affect the role of carriers and the decisions of shippers. Advanced robotics is making it possible for manufacturers in Europe and the United States to reshore production activities that had migrated to low-cost labor destinations. Digitization of freight logistics is enabling asset sharing and creating new players in the logistics chain. Several countries are conducting trials of autonomous rail and trucking. How these developments will affect traditional railways is a matter of keen interest among strategic decision makers.
- *Cross-chain control centers and synchromodality.* Cross-chain control centers (4Cs) and control towers bring together the latest technology, sophisticated software concepts, and supply chain professionals. The purpose of a 4C is to allow the joint control and coordination of one or more complex chains covering both physical and information and financial flows. Through the exchange, greater volumes can be bundled, increasing the options to use rail and inland shipping. The approach to asset sharing also facilitates joint decisions, which reduce inefficiencies. The benefits for participating parties are greater than they would be were the parties acting alone.

4C is closely linked to and supports the development of synchromodality, an integrated view of planning, booking, and management that uses different transport modes to provide flexibility in handling transport demand. The concept is synonymous with the creation of an optimal, flexible, and sustainable transport system in which companies can choose from a range of modalities at any time. Such a system ensures optimum transport combinations and allows companies to easily switch between modes if necessary.

NOTE

1. First-party logistics providers are shipper-owned logistics operations (truck fleets, warehousing facilities, and warehouse personnel). Second-party logistics (2PL) providers are asset-owning subcontractors (an example is a road hauler) that perform specific functions (such as trucking and warehousing). 3PL providers are non-asset-owning companies that coordinate transport, warehousing, and logistics services. Fourth-party logistics providers are system integrators that are contracted by the industry to plan and coordinate the whole supply chain, including coordination of 3PL and 2PL providers.

REFERENCES

AASHTO (American Association of State Highway and Transportation Officials). 2017. *Transportation: Investment in America: Freight-Rail Bottom Line Report.* Washington, DC: AASHTO.

Capgemini. 2018. *2018 Third-Party Logistics Study: The State of Logistics Outsourcing.* Paris: Capgemini.

Lieb, Robert C., and Brooks A. Bentz. 2004. "The Use of Third-Party Logistics Services by Large American Manufacturers: The 2003 Survey." *Transportation Journal* 43 (3): 24–33.

Lowe, David. 2005. *Intermodal Freight Transport.* New York: Elsevier.

Levinson, Marc. 2008. *The Box: How the Shipping Container Made the World Smaller and the World Economy Bigger.* Princeton, NJ: Princeton University Press.

3 Regaining Modal Share in a Changing World

This chapter discusses the experience of European and North American rail organizations that have taken steps in response to changes in transport and logistics.

REVIVING FREIGHT RAIL IN EUROPE AND NORTH AMERICA

Europe and North America have reduced—and in some cases reversed—the trend of declining modal share for freight. Railways in North America, particularly the United States, are arguably the most successful and competitive in the world. This was not always the case.

Rail freight accounted for more than 70 percent of intercity ton-miles in 1930, according to the Association of American Railroads (AAR 2018). By 1960, that share had fallen to just under 45 percent and, by 1980, was under 20 percent. The 1970s began with the bankruptcy of the Pennsylvania Central Railroad, the largest railway in the United States—then the largest corporate bankruptcy in U.S. history. Six other bankruptcies followed soon after. At one point, a fifth of the nation's track mileage was owned by bankrupt railways. The term "standing derailment" was coined to describe stationary freight cars that toppled over because the poorly maintained track underneath gave way (AAR 2015; Channon 2001).

Before 1980, rail freight transportation in the United States was heavily regulated. Government mandating of tariffs and service routing resulted in limited economies of scale in operations, because fragmentation in service delivery accompanied overcapacity (Breen 1982).

In 1980, the U.S. Congress passed the Staggers Rail Act, which deregulated many aspects of rail transport infrastructure development and service provision (Palley 2011). The act dramatically changed the environment in which railways operated by allowing much greater flexibility in setting prices and service levels. Before 1980, railways were expected to charge shippers the rates approved by the Interstate Commerce Commission—regardless of volume or customer. Delays in establishing new rates meant that the rates did not always keep up with inflation. Rail organizations were also prohibited from abandoning redundant low-density, financially nonviable lines.

Within five years of deregulation, the revival was evident, as rail freight volumes started increasing (figure 3.1). Between 1981 and 2009, the rail industry invested $510 billion in capital improvements and reduced the maintenance backlog. In addition, the return on investment grew, making rail a viable investment option. Trains running on better-maintained tracks proved safer: accident rates on freight rail dropped 65 percent between 1981 and 2009.

The natural advantages of geography and lack of political boundaries also favored U.S. railways. The absence of national borders between states promoted consistent regulations, such as safety and crew standards. Technological standardization in the North American network also played a crucial role by enabling long-haul rail to be economical. Crucially, the railways started focusing on the needs of customers and ways to offer customized services. With the new customer-focused mindset, and without regulation preventing adaptation, came increasing openness to intermodal opportunities. Restrictions that made it difficult to haul international freight in one direction and domestic in

FIGURE 3.1

U.S. freight railway productivity, volume, revenue, and rates, 1964–2017

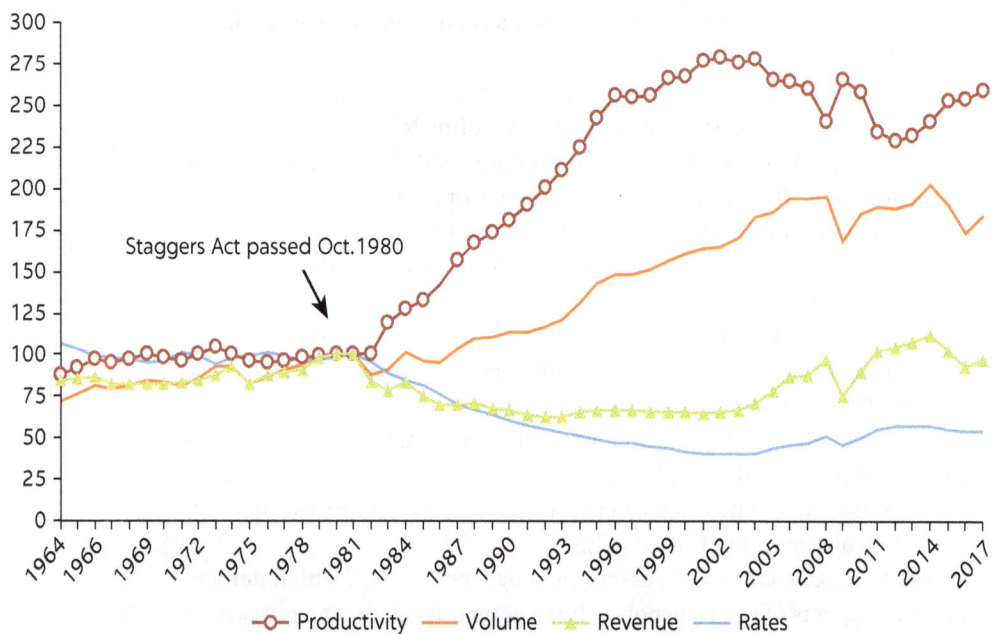

Source: Data from Association of American Railroads 2017.
Note: 1981 = 100. Rates are inflation-adjusted revenue per ton-mile. Volume is measured in ton-miles. Productivity is revenue ton-miles per constant dollar operating expense. The decline in productivity in recent years was caused largely by higher fuel prices in the productivity calculation.

the other were relaxed. New flexibility in pricing gave railways more options when pricing container traffic.

The situation was different in Canada, which is a vast and resource-intense country. Canada's relatively limited rail network focuses on moving bulk products, such as grain and wood. The main challenge has been better intercontinental logistics between the main gateway ports—Vancouver, Montreal, Prince Rupert, and Halifax. Canada's rail reforms and the sale of the Canadian National Railway for more than $2 billion in an initial public offering resulted in a highly competitive and low-cost rail sector. Tariffs declined, and service improved. Canadian National Railway operations now rank among the best for global railway financial performance. Rail sector investment in Canada has increased dramatically.

In the European Union (EU), less than 20 percent of inland freight moves by rail—down from 80 percent at the start of the 20th century.[1] Differences across countries are large. In the United Kingdom, for example, rail moves less than 10 percent of freight. The dramatic decline from almost 80 percent in the 1930s coincides with significant reforms of the 1980s and 1990s, when the rail sector was unbundled. The success or failure of British rail reforms has been widely debated, but the results include a huge increase in competition among the rail service providers that emerged from the reforms, significant increases in private investment in the rail freight sector, and substantial gains in rail freight market shares for individual carriers relative to the 1990s. It is unlikely the railways in the United Kingdom will regain the prominence they once held. Nevertheless, specialist freight still relies on rail for a key part of its logistics (Drew and Nash 2016).

In contrast, in Germany and the Netherlands, action by governments has played a critical role in the spin-off and revitalization of freight rail. In Germany railways have undergone—and arguably are still undergoing—a transition from inefficient and monopolistic state railways toward market-oriented enterprises as a byproduct of successful rail market liberalization. The transition was sparked by pressure from falling market shares and ever larger deficits in the context of tight state budgets.

Until the early 1990s, state-owned railways in East and West Germany were part of the ministries of transport. Reunification created the right environment for reform (box 3.1). In 1994, Deutsche Bahn AG was formed as a 100 percent state-owned but legally private enterprise that could act independently in the market and carry out the necessary changes in strategy and management. This corporatization, which involved restructuring of public enterprises into business corporations, made railway operations more profitable. Unnecessary overhead costs were cut, and the organizations formed were given more flexibility to respond to the market and customers. Although the state still cofinances investments in public rail infrastructure, state budgets are relieved of ongoing administrative costs. The German rail reform is a good example of how the necessary transition from a state organization to a private company can be managed without battles with unions and long-lasting strikes. The rights of incumbent civil servants remained untouched, with the obligations taken over by the state. High-skilled civil servants were leased to the new private rail company at market rates, with the cost difference borne by the state. New employees were engaged on new terms.

BOX 3.1

Transitioning from an inefficient to a modern, market-oriented railway sector in Germany

German rail faced massive challenges in the 1990s:

- Debt was heavy, and there was a need for public financing, dramatically increasing the risks for the state budget.
- Between 1950 and 1990, rail market share shrank from 37 percent to 6 percent for passenger transport and from 56 percent to 15 percent for cargo.
- Political economy and the lack of a legal framework for the railways reduced the operational effectiveness of civil servants.
- Increasing freight traffic and growing environmental awareness required a high-performing railway system.

The reform package introduced in 1994 transformed the sector:

- It created a new regulatory framework for railways, including changes in the constitution, seven new laws, and more than 130 changes to existing laws.
- It transformed two German railways into one state-owned joint stock company.
- The Federal State assumed the obligations of the new Deutsche Bahn AG, hiring the services of former civil servants.
- Civil servants kept their contracts with the Federal Railway State Property and were leased out at market rates to the new Deutsche Bahn AG

as needed; new employees were hired on market-competitive terms.

- One hundred eighty infrastructure projects were approved to renew the railway network.
- More than 100,000 employees and managers were retrained and given the opportunity to resume their careers in line with the new direction.
- Regional administration was replaced by business departments, as profit centers with regional dependencies.
- Cost accounting was adopted on the basis of business fields, freight type, and rail lines, which enabled transparency and market-oriented pricing.

The reforms yielded positive results:

- Between 1994 and 2012, passenger transport increased by 36 percent and freight traffic by 58 percent.
- Public cofinancing for railways fell from €20.5 billion in 1994 to €16.7 billion in 2012.
- Despite the traffic increase, carbon dioxide emissions decreased by 16 percent in passenger transport and by 10 percent in freight transport.
- Return on capital employed was 8.3 percent and company profit €1.5 billion in 2012.
- The number of employees fell from 372,000 in 1994 to 299,000 in 2012.
- Infrastructure was provided by Deutsche Bahn AG.
- Customer satisfaction rose.

SPECIALIZING IN TRADITIONAL "RAIL-FRIENDLY" TRAFFIC

Although intermodal transport is the fastest-growing freight type for railways in developed countries, the most successful railways began the turnaround in declining modal share by consolidating in traditional bulk transportation, where railway has a competitive advantage in moving large volumes over long distances at low costs (photograph 3.1). In this segment, block trains with specialized wagon equipment operate highly efficient shuttle services between origins and destinations. These services are often the core business for most successful railways, because they play to the strengths of rail-centric logistics.

PHOTOGRAPH 3.1

Wagon tipping for efficient unloading of coal from rail to barge, Königs Wusterhausen, Germany

Source: LUTRA, Königs Wusterhausen.

To meet the needs of customers, modern railways often adopt a matrix organization that complements their regional organization with cross-cutting key account management in the core business of the customer. For example, Deutsche Bahn AG differentiates business customers among automotive, construction materials, chemicals, industrial goods, intermodal, consumer goods, and iron, coal, and steel. To maintain customer focus and retain customers, it has dedicated sales teams with account management, regional support, and a central customer service office for each customer grouping. Railways in many developing countries no longer carry these freight types, which for many railways was the natural choice for shippers of bulk freight.

Another traditional rail-friendly market is conventional wagon load traffic, which is based on extensive shunting, consolidation, and disassembling of trains (single wagons or wagon groups). This kind of traffic is suited for smaller customers who do not have sufficient freight volumes to fill a block train. It was an important part of rail freight in Europe but progressively declined because it is slower, less reliable, less flexible, and usually more expensive than road traffic. As a result, service to private rail sidings ceased and rail connections closed in many countries, often resulting in a vicious circle of high costs, less cargo, and closure of sidings. Experience shows that revitalizing the system of single-wagon and group traffic requires the active involvement and cooperation of rail freight forwarders, rail ports for consolidation and dispatch to long distances, and shunting systems with modern automation and digitized marshalling operations (photograph 3.2 and box 3.2). Deutsche Bahn AG in Germany and several U.S. railways, such as BNSF and Norfolk Southern, have been relatively successful in revitalizing the wagon load segment.

Marshalling yard for consolidation of wagon loads

Source: © Norbert Wagener/World Bank. Permission required for reuse.

BOX 3.2

Increasing competitiveness by automating marshalling yards

To increase its competitiveness, DB Cargo is investing in the digitalization of its production centers—the marshalling yards. An important milestone is the conversion of locomotive shunting in the marshalling yard into a fully automated system that uses modern sensors and control technology to detect obstacles and people while automatically shunting freight cars. Its processes are embedded in the entire control of the marshalling yard. A pilot project is underway at the Munich North shunting station.

INCLUDING FREIGHT RAIL AS PART OF A TOTAL LOGISTICS SOLUTION

An important lesson from successful railways in Europe and the United States is the focus on improving operational efficiency and taking a holistic view of logistics from the perspectives of shippers, freight forwarders, and third-party logistics providers (3PLs). Doing so requires an understanding of the drivers of logistics costs for specific segments of the economy and types of freight.

Various studies in the United States show that reliability of service, price, travel time, flexibility of service, and control and security are critical. For rail to be part of a holistic logistics service, rail organizations must cultivate a reputation for efficient, competitive, and reliable services.

In many emerging economies, rail companies have traditionally had captive markets in mining and movement of bulk products owned by the public sector. With a captive market and less customer-centric orientation, rail organizations focused on building new infrastructure and paid less attention to understanding the market.

Some shippers in time-sensitive freight categories place reliability above price. Given the just-in-time operations that characterize logistics chains, even the fastest and least expensive transport service will not be attractive if it is unreliable. For containerizable freight, inventory costs are much more significant than transportation costs. The argument that rail is a cheaper alternative does not tip decisions of shippers.

For decades, efforts to address falling market share in rail organizations focused on improving internal processes and operations. The strategic plans of many rail organizations often make a strong case for the cost advantages of moving freight by rail (compared with road) and service-level advantages that come from efficiencies in rail service. The changing landscape of global logistics, in which several modes of transport may be involved in a supply chain, has forced successful organizations to rethink their approach by understanding the total logistics costs and actors and the drivers of decision making in the entire chain.

In most emerging economies, the various modes of surface transport are not integrated in a manner that allows synergies and complementarity. The fragmented networks—built before the major changes in logistics—are not equipped to meet rapidly rising freight traffic, changing consumption patterns, or the increasing numbers of production centers. Limited integrated planning and investment in freight transport has resulted in inefficiencies that have contributed to increasing logistics costs and that have curtailed the competitiveness of companies and sectors that depend on the efficiency of their logistics. In this context most shippers opted for trucking services, which despite obvious shortcomings provided a lower-risk alternative than railways.

In principle, all combinations of modes are possible, as figure 3.2 illustrates. In practice, the trade-off between transport and transshipment costs affects which modes are used. The larger the volume, the easier it is to create multimodal corridors with intermediate transshipments. The main challenge in

FIGURE 3.2

Optimized networks viewed through the lens of total logistics

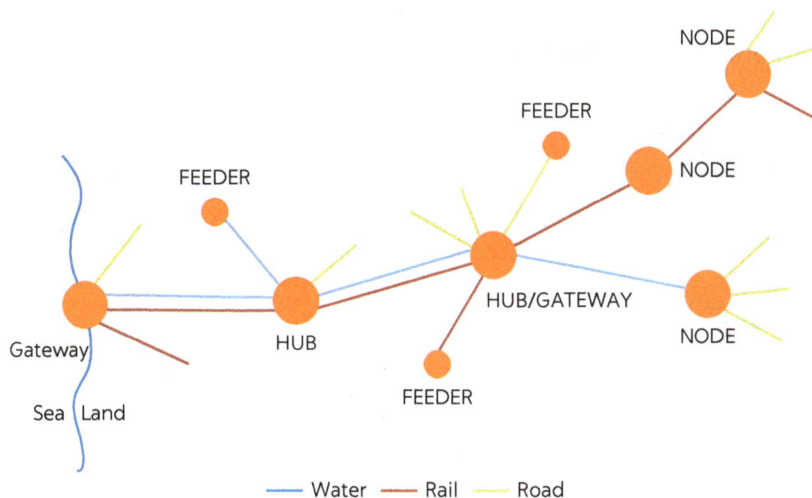

Source: STC-NESTRA 2015.

developing multimodal transport is to bundle cargo in such a way that massive flows are created on links of the corridors. Bundling freight is realized by locating activities that generate and attract cargo in the surroundings of the nodes (inland ports) and aligning continental and the massive maritime-oriented flows. Rail is needed as an alternative in case of problems on the waterways and vice versa. In this sense railways play an important complementary role for inland ports, enlarging their geographic reach and scope and providing access to local plants and distribution centers.

For such an integrated system to be successful, critical hubs must be created to consolidate or generate sufficiently large volumes of freight. Figures 3.3 and 3.4 illustrate the transitions required for rail to play a role in overall logistics.

In a multimodal point-to-point network (figure 3.3a)—typical of most transport networks in emerging economies—the opportunities to bundle freight are limited. However, when strategic hubs are created as shown in figure 3.3b, then sufficient volumes can be generated to allow for rail centered logistics. In practice, this requires much more analysis on location and discussions with shippers and the supply chain to design service requirements to suit

FIGURE 3.3

Transition from current to desired transport configuration

a. Multimodal point-to-point network

b. Intermodal integrated network

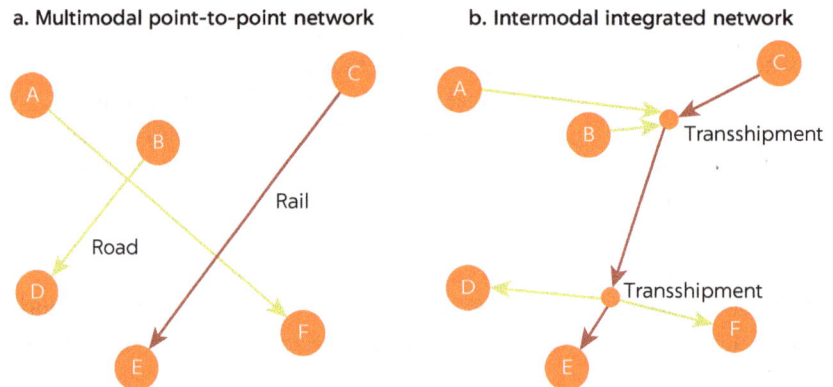

Source: Data from World Bank 2018.

FIGURE 3.4

Responding to the need for total logistics

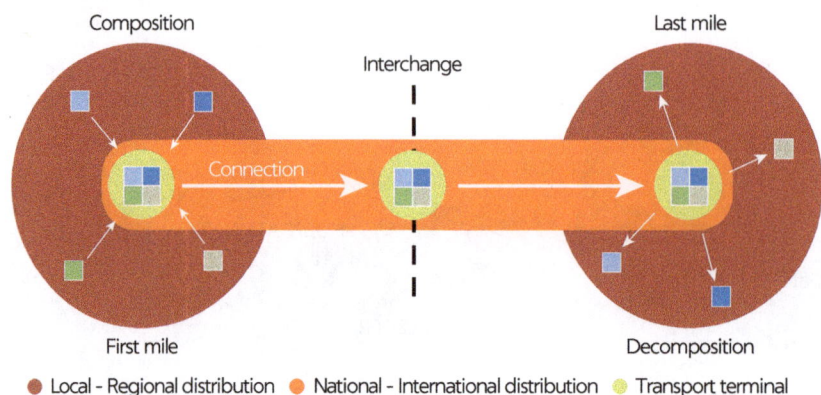

● Local - Regional distribution ● National - International distribution ● Transport terminal

Source: Data from World Bank 2018.

operations requirements. Carefully thought needs to be given to how to combine flows in both directions.

In countries with relatively integrated logistics and transport networks, the concepts of composition and decomposition initially centered on trying to optimize processing and transshipment of bulk raw materials. The location and design of terminals responded to improvements in economic efficiency. Terminals were built to package these bulk commodities in a load break function for heavy industrial activities. These types of terminals generally require huge investments in infrastructure and need to be located at strategic points of modal convergence. Railways offered a natural and cost-effective surface transport mode to link terminals.

Internationally, integrated logistics has become the preferred logistics solution for shippers and major freight customers—especially for time or cost-sensitive cargo. In the United States, for example, truck driver shortages, unpredictable fuel prices, and implementation of new government policies that restrict hours of service on the road have contributed to truck capacity challenges for large customers. Shippers are always looking for ways to cut costs and improve services. Rail-oriented intermodal logistics offers options that U.S. railroad companies have responded to with attractive service offerings.

In the EU, a policy shift toward decreasing the share of freight volume moving by truck in favor of water and rail has been a key driver of intermodal transport (boxes 3.3 and 3.4). The combination of rapid growth in trade among EU countries and insufficient infrastructure has created fears of increased traffic congestion, logistics bottlenecks, and environmental problems. Hence, in addition to heavy investments in intermodal systems and infrastructure by individual countries, the EU has developed several trans-European intermodal corridors with a strong emphasis on logistics services and well-connected hubs, such as the Duisburg multimodal hub shown in photograph 3.3.

BOX 3.3

Reinventing freight rail as part of a total logistics service in Europe

The share of rail in freight traffic in most European countries has fallen consistently since the mid-20th century: in most countries, rail now accounts for about 10–20 percent of total freight moved. Road haulage is the preferred mode for most customers, because road-based logistics are inherently flexible, agile, cost competitive, and reliable.

An emerging trend is for transport services to be integrated as part of the overall logistics system of customers (storage, materials handling, and supply chain management). Most large customers now demand one-stop-shop logistics, leading to the emergence of huge haulers. Such solutions create opportunities for rail freight organizations in Europe to contribute to integrated logistics packages, in which rail freight operators partner with other organizations to provide seamless services—total logistics from door to door.

For example, DHL Supply Chain, one of the world's largest logistics companies, manages just-in-time operations to support various car manufacturers. Its services include managing inbound logistics for manufacturing materials and constituent service parts. For one European auto manufacturer, DHL Supply Chain coordinates the movement of 60,000 components from 27 suppliers on three continents into a strategic assembly facility every day, collecting from suppliers, sorting, and delivering 2,500 items per hour to production lines. This approach has reduced the cost of production for the auto manufacturer by 25 percent in three years.

Reinventing port-centered intermodal transport in Rotterdam

The Port of Rotterdam is the largest port in Europe and a consolidated global hub. Its rise to prominence is rooted in improved intermodal transport. Although modal share has not changed much, the overall volume of traffic has increased several-fold.

The infrastructure and operations development strategy of the port and its institutional reorganization have increased throughput and improved port financial performance. These two indicators constitute a proxy for the value this development represents for the final customer. Development of hinterland connections and access from the port to the major freight transport routes in Europe has helped consolidate the advantage of the port. Port customers value the availability of different options for transportation; the quality of the connections for planning routes, accessibility, and travel time; and the frequency of services.

To expand the capacity and scope of logistics services, the Port of Rotterdam (and several other seaports in Europe) have designed extended gates that move some traditional port functions to inland locations. The inland terminal at Venlo has several dedicated rail shuttles that provide scheduled services between the Port of Rotterdam and the terminal. Many port-related services are now delivered at Venlo rather than Rotterdam, and clients engage with the terminal services as they would with the port.

PHOTOGRAPH 3.3

Logistics terminal in Duisburg, Germany, integrating multiple modes to meet customers' needs

Source: © Harrie De Leijer/World Bank. Permission required for reuse.

ADOPTING INNOVATIVE LOGISTICS SOLUTIONS AND INFRASTRUCTURE FOR BUNDLING FREIGHT

The full range of logistics services that shippers are looking for presents opportunities for rail organizations to develop different models for engagement. Freight transport is increasingly subsumed within the overall process of logistics (storage, materials handling, and supply chain management). These value-added services create opportunities to increase margins and volume for rail organizations that can adapt to changes in logistics.

BOX 3.5

Creating opportunities for railways: Case study of the Nuremberg freight village

A freight village (FV) is an organized, specialized industrial estate at which logistics companies can colocate. to provide value-added services. Their development is usually led by regional or national governments. To be successful, FVs requires strong leadership and vision from the public sector to build partnerships and make targeted investments in strategic locations that will attract companies that benefit from better logistics.

FV Nuremberg ranks among the top three European freight villages (after Verona, Italy, and Bremen, Germany), thanks to its performance, maturity, and innovative concepts. It is an integral part of achieving large volumes of cargo and using multimodal transport.

The FV benefits from a central geographical location within east–west and north–south European traffic flows. It is connected to all transport modes and offers intermodal long-distance connections to major seaports in Europe and large industrial centers in Europe and Asia. The major European seaports of Rotterdam, Hamburg, and Trieste are 600–700 kilometers away (15–18 hours by train). A weekly train to China connects Nuremberg with Chengdu in 17 days. A rail line between the FV railway station and the Nuremberg marshalling yard (three kilometers away) links the FV with the main rail route from Munich to Berlin and the national and European rail network. For the regional industry and the FV tenants, these multimodal connections offer the full range of options for every logistics demand in terms of quality, time, and costs.

Global logistics firms such as DHL, DB Schenker, Kuehne & Nagel, and others have located in the FV. Although they are competitors, they collaborate and supplement each other in various ways, allowing all of them to benefit from optimized and reduced logistics costs.

Two hundred logistics-related companies operate in FV Nuremberg, directly employing 6,700 people. More than 20,000 indirect jobs have also been created in the region of Nuremberg. The FV acts as a logistics center for industry in the Nuremberg Metropolitan Region, offering full logistics services of international transport and local delivery, warehousing, contract logistics, and value-adding services (packaging, stuffing, stripping, repair, sorting, labelling, assembling, and reverse logistics).

Part of the attraction of the FV is its integrated infrastructure, which consists of intermodal handling facilities, port-related industries, specialized facilities for logistics service providers, customs clearance, and various auxiliary services. All the terminals are designed to meet the needs of industries in clusters called productive neighborhoods. Multipurpose terminals for bulk and break-bulk commodities, which are equipped with rail-mounted gantry cranes and elevators for grain and fertilizers, can transship on the quayside directly between ship, rail, and road. The multimodal container terminal handles containers of all types, swap bodies, and semitrailers; serves rail, road, and water transport; and includes service facilities for containers. The FV also has a multimodal heavy lift terminal for the transshipment of heavy and out-of-gauge cargo (up to 550 tons, mainly Siemens transformers).

For other logistics companies, the FV provides rail and road connectivity and facilities in warehousing, international forwarding, domestic trucking, courier, parcel and express, distribution of fast-moving consumer goods for the region, contract logistics, sea and air freight, and other services. Because of the FV's excellent location, several companies act as regional or European hubs within a hub-and-spoke system.

Management of the FV is based on the publicly owned landlord model. The port holding company of the Federal State of Bavaria (Bayernhafen GmbH) owns the land and the port-handling facilities. Bayernhafen GmbH, together with the city of Nuremberg and Roth-Hafen Nurnberg Roth GmbH, created a management company to manage the port and the FV. The management company develops and leases the land plots and offers various services for tenants, including provision of crane drivers. It acts as a site and service architect. A separate company for the operation of the multimodal terminal was established, of which DUSS GmbH, a subsidiary of Deutsche Bahn, is a shareholder and with which it is actively involved.

FORMING NONTRADITIONAL PARTNERSHIPS INVOLVING RAILWAYS

Competition between parties in the logistics chain and issues of confidentiality often result in a lack of willingness to cooperate and share information. The result is often fragmented services that do not generate the critical mass needed for efficient and high-quality intermodal solutions for which rail is a backbone.

The challenge for railways is how to ensure that the rail component is included in door-to-door-logistics solutions. Railways can either become active as 3PLs through affiliated companies, or they can form nontraditional partnerships with other companies. Several examples in the United States and Europe show how it is possible for railways to play a critical role by forming nontraditional partnerships.

Railways in North America have heavily engaged 3PLs to increase intermodal volumes. They collaborate with large trucking companies, which are increasingly taking on the role of 3PL for their clients. Firms like Schneider National, J.B. Hunt, and United Parcel Service have become some of the biggest rail transport customers. The trucking companies benefit by being able to provide their shipper customers with lower quotes and by relieving some of the pressure created by the driver shortage. The railways benefit by acquiring new business, particularly from shippers that might have been reluctant to manage an intermodal supply chain on their own. Shippers that may have been reluctant to deal with the complexity of modal connections on their own are often happy to have a 3PL manage it for them. Shippers may also have reservations about the reliability of rail but may be willing to trust their 3PL to make it work. In such cases, the railways benefit from needing to win over only one 3PL to gain traffic from multiple shippers who trust that 3PL.

One prominent and longstanding relationship between a railroad and a trucking company is the partnership between the BNSF Railway Company (the largest freight railroad network in North America) and J.B. Hunt. The partnership began in 1989, with the loading of a J.B. Hunt trailer onto an Atchison, Topeka, and Santa Fe Railway train (a BNSF predecessor). Initially, 150 trailers moved between California and Chicago. The relationship then grew with increasing volumes and geographic scope. Both J.B. Hunt and BNSF made strategic investments in intermodal facilities and aligned operations. At various business promotion events, J.B. Hunt emphasizes its location adjacent to BNSF and promotes its proximity to efficient last-mile services. Box 3.6 describes how one company benefitted from the partnership between BNSF and J.B. Hunt.

BNSF's share of containerizable freight has grown in consumer products, opening up new opportunities for sustainable rail market share (figure 3.5). The consumer products freight business provided about a third of the company's freight revenues for the 12 months ended December 31, 2017. It consisted of three business sectors: international intermodal; domestic intermodal (including truckload-intermodal marketing companies and expedited truckload–less-than-truckload–parcel); and automotive.

BNSF is by no means alone in building relationships with trucking companies and 3PLs. Because North American railways are regional in coverage, it makes sense for large 3PLs and trucking companies to work with multiple railways. Schneider National, for example, has alliances with five major North American railways. J.B. Hunt complements BNSF's western network with a partnership with Norfolk Southern in the east.

Using a third-party logistics provider and rail transport to improve logistics at Petco

One intermodal customer to find BNSF through J.B. Hunt was Petco, a pet supply retailer operating more than 1,000 stores in 50 states, with 10 distribution centers operating behind the scenes. Petco was seeking to reduce its transportation costs and mitigate its environmental impact. Through J.B. Hunt, with which it had a close relationship, Petco agreed to participate in a pilot intermodal program starting in 2008. Petco was happy with the service reliability during the three-month pilot, prompting a shift toward heavier use of intermodal transport across its distribution network, even for time-sensitive deliveries to stores. The $60 billion a year U.S. pet supply business is extremely competitive, with margins that are sensitive to logistics costs. Petco reduced its use of private fleets and narrowed the number of carriers it works with, directing much of its shipment volume to J.B. Hunt to manage.

FIGURE 3.5

Revenues of BNSF by business group, 2000–17

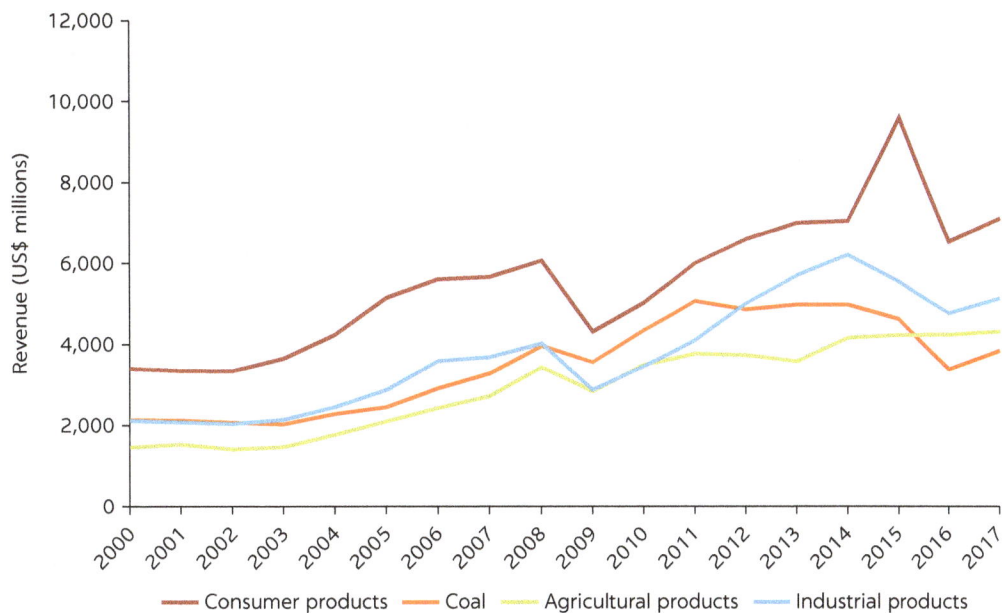

Source: Data from BNSF annual reports.

CSX partnered with Yusen Logistics to serve the needs of a leading food ingredient company. When the company sought to reduce transportation costs for its nondairy creamer, Yusen Logistics recommended an intermodal logistics configuration and helped allay the reservations of the shipper and its customers by offering to package the services and remain the single-entry point. CSX engineers devised a special loading pattern to avoid damage to the dairy products. Through this proposal Yusen Logistics reduced the landed costs of the product by half while meeting customer service requirements. Initial intermodal volumes were shipments to customers; the company also planned to use intermodal transport for shipments between plants.

BOX 3.7

Shipping fresh produce from Chengdu to Moscow by train

In February 2018, DB Schenker, one of the world's leading logistics service providers, operated the first block train moving 11 reefer containers carrying fresh produce from Chengdu to Moscow, a distance of some 6,000 miles. The block train carried 160 tons of perishable agricultural products for Rollink, a large China-based business-to-business food trading company. To deliver the fresh vegetables to customers shortly after arrival in Moscow, DB Schenker handles customs clearances and local distribution, providing services from port to door. The shift away from the traditional air-based logistics is expected to lead to significant cost savings.

Box 3.7 describes a block train service from Chengdu to Moscow, which follows a similar logistics service model to that proposed by Yusen and CSX for food products.

Analyzing logistics chains and exploring how rail can be slotted into strategic freight types by partnering with trucking companies, 3PLs, and freight forwarders can open new opportunities for railways in emerging economies on the basis of alignment of strengths and inherent advantages. Realizing these opportunities requires understanding the needs of customers. It requires a shift away from the traditional paradigm in emerging economies, which focuses on improving internal services and operations without trying to understand the logistics bottlenecks of customers.

DEVELOPING IN-HOUSE LOGISTICS CAPABILITIES

North American railways have not limited themselves to depending on 3PLs to bring in new intermodal volumes. All large North American railways have formed at least one subsidiary to provide logistics services. These services range from transloading to coordinating drayage (the transport of goods over a short distance) to supply chain consulting.

Railways often have multiple subsidiaries with different market or functional focuses. By coordinating or operating drayage services and taking on the role of 3PLs themselves, railways can form stronger direct relationships with major shippers and increase their share of supply chain spending.

In contrast to many other transportation businesses, including passenger rail, freight railways typically have a small customer base. As a result, they can afford to develop deep relationships and customize their approaches to winning the most valuable business through value-adding services and flexibility.

BNSF's level of engagement with 3PLs did not prevent it from forming BNSF Logistics (BNSFL), a subsidiary that describes itself as a 3PL (box 3.8).

Union Pacific Railroad has also formed multiple logistics subsidiaries. In 2001, it formed Insight Network Logistics to manage the delivery of vehicles from assembly plants to dealers. Its initial client was Chrysler, though the company markets its services to the broader auto industry. Chrysler chooses its carriers, but Insight Network Logistics tracks and coordinates shipments, with the goal of reducing transportation time and cutting Chrysler's inventory holding costs.

BOX 3.8

Expanded service offerings at BNSF

BNSF founded BNSF Logistics (BNSFL) in 2002 to include third-party logistics in the range of services it offers. BNSFL coordinates supply chains across multiple modes, including rail, road, and sea transportation. It has managed relationships with large clients, including Amazon, which awarded a contract to BNSFL in 2006 to manage freight movements between domestic suppliers and Amazon's North American distribution network. BNSFL has worked in the brick and mortar retail space as well, helping a large European retailer ship goods to its distribution network in North America from vendors in Mexico

through intermodal freight. It also organized the movement of potatoes for Frito-Lay (a leader in the snack business), using refrigerated trailers on flatcars to move the potatoes to Chicago and then by highway to a processing plant in Frankfort, Indiana.

BNSFL has also sought to cultivate a niche market for wind turbine transportation. It has developed its own technology and acquired several transportation technology services firms since 2015. To handle oversized and complex cargo, particularly wind turbines, the company designed special cars and assists in loading and inspection.

To complement Insight Network Logistics' movement of new cars, Union Pacific formed ShipCarsNow to manage the movement of used cars. It also formed Streamline to manage intermodal shipments, including coordination of drayage. Streamline does not limit itself to using the Union Pacific rail network. It advertises its connections with the Norfolk Southern and CSX railroad networks, both of which operate primarily east of the Mississippi River, complementing Union Pacific's western network. Photograph 3.4 shows a heavy-lift block train, a service typically offered by U.S. railways.

In the eastern United States, both Norfolk Southern and CSX have formed their own intermodal subsidiaries, in addition to working with Union Pacific's Streamline. CSX Intermodal Terminals, a subsidiary of CSX, owns and operates intermodal terminals and performs drayage services for certain customers. Norfolk Southern's Thoroughbred Direct Intermodal Services provides door-to-door intermodal services in the United States and Mexico. Its customers include 3PLs as well as ocean shipping lines and trucking companies.

Norfolk Southern also has a separate subsidiary, Triple Crown Services, which uses trailers called RoadRailers, which are designed to run on rails without the use of flatcars. The trailers are transferred onto rail bogies using their air-ride suspensions in a few minutes, without the need for lifting or cranes. The trailers need to be specially built, both to connect to the bogies and to withstand the 200-ton tension and compression forces experienced when part of a 125-trailer train is connected. The volumes moved by Triple Crown rose from 136,000 loads in 1992, to 266,000 loads in 2002, to 294,000 in 2017.

Norfolk Southern has also invested significantly in providing customized solutions for its customers. When BMW was searching for a site for its U.S. operations in the early 1990s, Norfolk Southern worked with local development officials to actively promote Greer, South Carolina as the site. The South Carolina Ports Authority owned a piece of property along the line; Norfolk Southern partnered with the ports authority to construct and operate an inland port, with Norfolk Southern providing rail infrastructure to support the project. Norfolk Southern's subsidiary Thoroughbred Direct Intermodal Services

Heavy-lift harvesting machines on a block train

Source: © Norfolk Southern. Used with permission; further permission required for reuse.

managed intermodal traffic, and the ports authority owned and operated the inland port.

BMW cites Norfolk Southern rail services as a factor in locating its facility in Greer. BMW uses containers to ship parts from Charleston to Greer and from Greer to Charleston, in preparation for export. It also uses the rail line to export finished vehicles. The rail service connects 235 miles using double-stack containers, using the same trains to serve multiple markets (photograph 3.5). BMW estimates that the rail service takes 20,000–25,000 trucks off Interstate 26 annually. The link also provides hub-and-spoke delivery services to various warehouses and distribution centers, including a tire manufacturer, a leading apparel distributor, and a chemical company. The impact of improvements in Norfolk Southern is evident in operational revenues as shown in figure 3.6.

Norfolk Southern has provided similar services for Ford, which started when Ford was debuting its vans in the United States. The unique service involved modifying the railcars by raising the middle deck in order to accommodate the transport of larger vans on the first level and shorter vehicles on the top level. Norfolk Southern developed a prototype, which it tested near Ford's Detroit headquarters. Norfolk Southern has also expanded and positioned its rail services within the logistics chains of nontraditional shippers. Using the advantages of containerization, it prepared a logistics package to move soybeans to Asia. Norfolk Southern transports large volumes of grain, but typically by bulk. For this shipper of soybeans, providing a clear chain of custody to ensure purity was essential, something that is much easier to achieve with containers. With a single point of responsibility, Norfolk Southern offered a competitive value proposition.

Double-stack container train

Source: © Norfolk Southern. Used with permission; further permission required for reuse.

FIGURE 3.6
Operating revenues of the Norfolk Southern Railway by market group, 2000–17

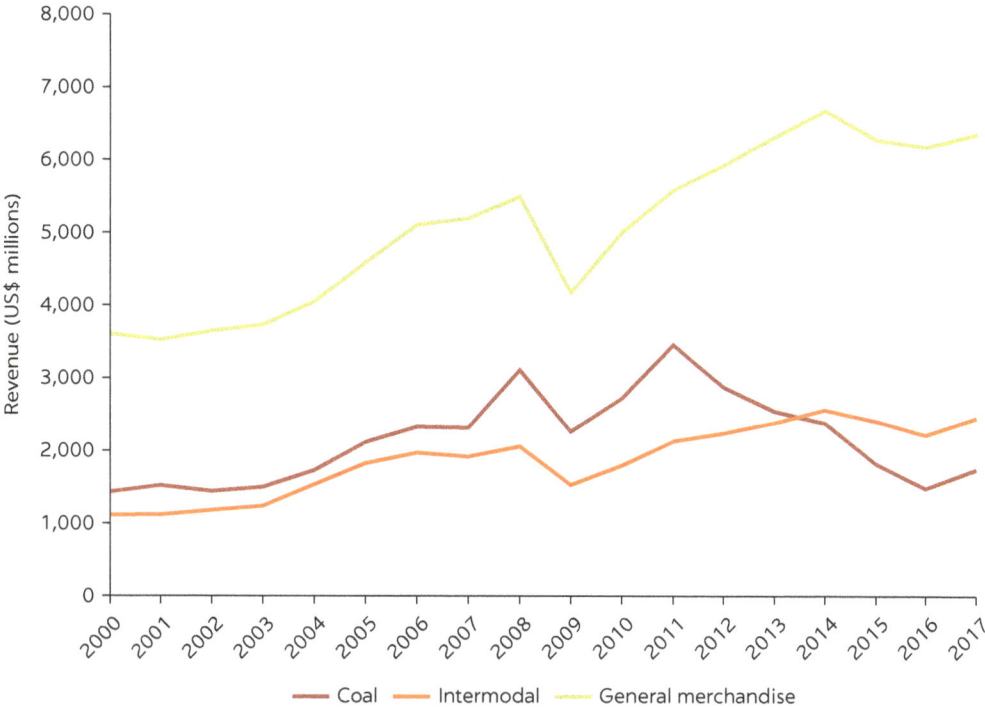

Source: Data from Norfolk Southern annual reports.

BOX 3.9

Leading rail-based logistics in Europe: DB Schenker

DB Schenker—the world's leading global logistics provider—is a remarkable example of how responding to changing logistics can reposition railroad organizations within a wider logistics chain. The product of a merger between Deutsche Bahn railroad and the Schenker forwarding company, the company provides a range of services for various industries, including automotive, aerospace and defense, beverages, consumer products, electronics, retail goods, health care and pharmaceuticals, and perishables. In addition to traditional logistics services for land, air, and ocean freight, DB Schenker provides contract logistics services for production, fulfillment, aftermarket, e-commerce, and value addition; fourth-party lead logistics services; and specialized services for events, fairs, exhibitions, and relocation services.

Norfolk Southern also works with Federal Express (FedEx), which chose it as the preferred eastern rail carrier for its FedEx Freight Priority and FedEx Freight Economy LTL services.

Rail freight modal shares in Europe have fallen, but some operators have successfully targeted the intermodal segment. Box 3.9 summarizes the experience of DB Schenker, which has developed a range of services comparable to those of U.S. railways.

In the United Kingdom, Freightliner (the second-largest rail freight operator in the country) expanded its intermodal line of business and entered into partnership with Genesee & Wyoming, a U.S. short-line railroad holding company that owns or maintains an interest in 120 railroads in Australia, Belgium, Canada, the Netherlands, the United Kingdom, and the United States. The partnership is now the largest rail operator in the United Kingdom and also owns a fleet of more than 250 trucks that perform drayage services and deliver up to 800 containers a day. The company also offers other ancillary services to customers, mainly shipping companies, including container storage and refurbishment and shipment tracking.

Through partnerships with shipping lines and the Port of Antwerp, Infrabel (a government-owned public limited company that builds, owns, maintains, and upgrades the Belgian railway network) has taken advantage of investments by the EU in rail tracks to present logistics solutions that have both business and environmental benefits. Investments in inland hubs in strategic locations have now made Infrabel a preferred partner for many shippers.

INVESTING IN LOGISTICS TECHNOLOGY AND INTERMODAL DIGITAL PLATFORMS

To remain relevant to intermodal logistics chains, reduce costs, and improve services for customers, railways have invested in various technologies. In North America there is a split between containers and piggybacking of trailers. Double stacking of containers is common and expanding for various freight types. Piggybacking provides flexibility for intermodal services and is increasingly used by several operators. According to the Association of American Railroads (AAR 2018), in 2017, about 88 percent of intermodal freight for North America was shipped in containers and 12 percent was shipped in trailers.

In Europe, diverse technologies have been introduced to improve operational efficiency. One example is swap body technology (photograph 3.6). Swap bodies are similar to containers but are typically not built to the same strength standards, making them lighter but impossible to stack. They are typically lifted from the bottom as opposed to the top. Few shippers outside Europe and the United States use swap bodies.

As rail organizations and governments invest in rail infrastructure, they will continue to face decisions about which technologies to invest in. Each has advantages and disadvantages. For example, although piggybacking allows railways to share trailers with the trucking industry, not all trailers are built strongly enough to be lifted onto trains (photograph 3.7).

Piggybacking has the disadvantage of requiring the railroad to transport wheels and axles, which add both height and weight (photograph 3.8). Swap bodies remove these disadvantages by separating the cargo from the undercarriage, but they do so at the expense of decreased compatibility with the trucking fleet. Neither trailers nor swap bodies are compatible with ocean shipping, which typically requires much stronger containers for stacking. Standard shipping containers are compatible with ocean shipping, and they improve efficiency when stacked on trains, requiring fewer cars per unit of load (increasing energy efficiency and reducing asset requirements). Double-stacked trains are also shorter, requiring shorter sidings. The height of two containers often exceeds available clearances, however, especially where there are overhead lines on electrical railroads. The added strength of shipping containers also adds weight.

As railways and governments continue their investment in rail infrastructure, it will be increasingly important to design infrastructure with intermodal movements in mind, avoiding incompatibilities wherever practical. When selecting the forms of intermodal infrastructure to invest in, it is important to consider the modes with which the railroad will be connecting, cost efficiencies, and retrofits that might be required to existing infrastructure.

PHOTOGRAPH 3.6

Swap bodies used to improve operational efficiency

Source: © World Bank. Permission required for reuse.

PHOTOGRAPH 3.7
Piggybacking of a container on a rail line

Source: © World Bank. Permission required for reuse.

PHOTOGRAPH 3.8
Intermodal freight—including piggybacking, single-stacked containers, and double-stacked containers—on a BNSF train in California

Source: © World Bank. Permission required for reuse.

In North America, railways make many of their own investments in infrastructure. Large railways have been investing in intermodal infrastructure. The focus is apparent in annual reports, which feature both progress and plans for intermodal traffic. For example, Norfolk Southern's 2017 annual report emphasizes the advantages of the intermodal network, which is described as the "most extensive intermodal network in the eastern half of the United States" (Norfolk Southern 2018). Norfolk Southern has invested heavily in the Crescent

Corridor, which spans 11 states from New Jersey to Louisiana. It has mobilized extensive financing from the private sector and institutional investors while also taking advantage of federal and state funding for upgrades to the Heartland Corridor, which connects Chicago to Virginia. The project received more than $83 million from the federal government and $10 million from states that are beneficiaries, with Norfolk Southern investing nearly $100 million toward the cost of clearing the corridor for double stacking. The project involved enlarging 28 tunnels through the Appalachian Mountains, some of which were constructed more than 100 years ago. The line, which was built to haul coal, needed to remain in operation for that purpose, but Norfolk Southern took the risk of disruptions for the potential improvements to its intermodal service. Double-stacked trains traveling from Virginia to Chicago saved up to two days of transit time.

SUMMARY OF LESSONS FOR RAIL ORGANIZATIONS IN EMERGING ECONOMIES

The experiences of rail organizations in North America and Europe provide several lessons for emerging economies:

- Implement modern management concepts, and make rail a customer-oriented business.
- Focus on the core offering of rail, with specialization and standardization for seamless logistics.
- Invest in innovative solutions and infrastructure that play to the strengths of railways.
- Develop a strategy for one-stop-shop logistics through full-service packages or collaboration with nontraditional partners; be open to intermediation by established logistics service providers that can consolidate freight, manage terminals, and allow rail to concentrate on core rail economics.
- Gain a detailed understanding of logistics chains and cost drivers for core customers, in order to (1) segment the transport market into natural flow categories, such as bulk export, mineral export, domestic minerals, industrial siding-to-siding business, and high-value intermodal (domestic and international) fast-moving consumer goods; (2) determine what the natural rail competitive spaces are for each of these flow categories; and (3) define what would be needed to compete and be successful in each category.
- Be alert to trends shaping national and global logistics.

NOTE

1. Eurostat. https://ec.europa.eu/eurostat/statistics-explained/index.php?title=Transport.

REFERENCES

AAR (Association of American Railroads). 2018. *A Short History of U.S. Freight Railroads.* Washington, DC: AAR. https://www.aar.org/wp-content/uploads/2018/05/AAR-Short-History-American-Freight-Railroads.pdf.

Breen, Denis A. 1982. *Regulatory Reform and the Trucking Industry: An Evaluation of the Motor Carrier Act* of 1980. Federal Trade Commission, Washington, DC.

Channon, Geoffrey, 2001. "Railways in Britain and the United States 1830–1940." In *Studies in Economic and Business History*. Burlington, VT: Ashgate.

Drew, Jeremy, and Chris Nash. 2016. *Vertical Separation of Railway Infrastructure: Does It Always Make Sense?* Institute for Transport Studies University of Leeds, Leeds, United Kingdom.

Norfolk Southern. 2018. *2017 Annual Report and 10-K*. Norfolk, VA: Norfolk Southern.

Palley, Joel. 2011. *Impact of the Staggers Rail Act of 1980.* https://www.fra.dot.gov/eLib/Details /L03012.

STC-NESTRA. 2015. *Platform for Multimodality and Logistics in Inland Ports*. Rotterdam: STC-NESTRA. https://ec.europa.eu/transport/sites/transport/files/modes/inland/doc/2015 -07-logistics-inland-ports-platform-long-position-paper.pdf.

4 What Can Policy Makers Do to Facilitate Modal Shift or Reverse the Declining Trend?

A discussion of modal share would be incomplete without highlighting ways in which policy makers can help promote rail logistics. A range of policy instruments beyond investments in infrastructure can be used to influence modal choice. Policy makers at various levels of local and central governments can use a combination of these instruments to overcome barriers, address market failures, and create opportunities for increased use of rail freight.

Rail freight transportation is especially competitive when cargo can be consolidated and flows matched to reach critical volumes over relatively long distances. Policy makers can facilitate such consolidation in several ways.

CHAMPIONING INSTITUTIONAL AND REGULATORY REFORMS THAT FOCUS ON THE CUSTOMER

Policy makers can support institutional and regulatory reforms that allow inefficient and monopolistic state railways to transition toward market-oriented enterprises that are responsive to various customers. A key ingredient for reviving rail modal share in Europe and the United States was adoption of the right regulatory and institutional environments. The most fundamental change brought about by freight rail deregulation in the United States was a paradigm shift from a focus on guaranteeing service availability to a focus on providing services to customers. Rate and service-level flexibility brought about by deregulation enabled railways in the United States to be more customer-centric.

There is no formula for how these reforms are managed—the experience in Germany and the Netherlands shows different paths to achieving the same objectives, with a stronger role for corporate enterprises that are as customer-oriented as the U.S. railways. But reform efforts in both Europe and the United States indicate that a core prerequisite for internal reform is the creation of the right mindset, institutional structure, and skills to focus first on achieving the core business of providing reliable rail infrastructure and efficient operations that are responsive to needs of customers.

A key enabler of innovation and customer responsiveness in North America has been specialization, particularly for the rail intermodal segment of the market. Rail reforms have allowed railways to specialize and divest themselves of noncore activities. In Europe and the United States, successful rail organizations reorganized to win back rail-friendly freight, mainly bulk products moving long distances or freight for which logistics are traditionally well suited for rail, such as movements from mine to port, silo to silo, siding to siding, or large warehouses to similar warehouses. These traditional markets have been lost in many countries. With the right institutional arrangements—customer service departments, dedicated account managers, customized service offerings—they can be regained. The same principles apply to wagon-load customers whose freight requires consolidation.

Containerized freight presents a slightly different challenge. The ecosystem includes new actors in the logistics chain—third-party logistics providers and similar intermediaries that have taken over the shipment origination–retail segment of the intermodal transport value chain through specialization. These nimble firms use technology to optimize freight shipments across carriers' networks and fleets on behalf of individual beneficiary cargo owners. They have allowed railways to specialize in the core business of end-to-end efficient operations.

USING SPATIAL PLANNING AND LAND USE MEASURES TO ENCOURAGE THE CLUSTERING AND SETTLEMENT OF LOGISTICS ACTIVITIES CLOSE TO RAIL

Through urban planning, zoning regulations, and building permits, governments control the use of land, which directly affects the private creation of logistics assets, such as intermodal terminals and warehouses. Land use in urban areas

---

BOX 4.1

Creation of a massive logistics park in Zaragoza, Spain

The government of the Autonomous Community of Aragón (CAA) planned to transform Zaragoza into the most important city for logistics in Europe by implementing PLAZA, a 10-year project to be completed by 2010. The objective was to prevent companies from leaving Spain for other European countries, create jobs, attract investment, and diversify the region's economic base.

In February 2000, the CAA presented its proposal to open a logistics park in Zaragoza. In October 2005, after an initial investment of more than €170 million, the government opened the largest logistics park in Europe for business.

The park exploited Zaragoza's geostrategic location as a door to Europe through the Pyrenees. A mixed public and private company oversaw the project and combined several policy instruments:

Land use measures. The company created a dry port through agreements with Spain's major ports to overcome the fact that Zaragoza is landlocked. This inland terminal connects directly to a seaport, reducing congestion at ports. A managerial park includes office space and a commercial area that encouraged the colocation of various companies.

Infrastructure spending. Spain's central government invested heavily in a high-speed passenger connection, which relieved pressure on existing infrastructure so that it could be used exclusively for cargo. France and Spain also laid out plans to construct a new tunnel for freight rail to cross the Pyrenees.

Knowledge management. PLAZA hosted a research and teaching institution to bring together knowledge of the supply chain from academia, industry, and government. The objective was to use the park as a collaborative experiment.

has a symbiotic relationship with the nature of the transportation system, something governments need to consider when setting policy objectives. Land use around ports and terminals is important for developing industry that can rely on this infrastructure.

Land use planning requires looking to the long term and anticipating future needs. Proactive policy making is required to make the best use of scarce land. Zoning can enable development of rail infrastructure links close to where freight is generated, allowing for densification of freight. Logistics zones on the outskirts of cities can combine warehousing and truck parking facilities. Governments can also use compulsory purchase orders to buy up land to be used for infrastructure development or to widen or reroute roads, rail, and waterways. These solutions are designed to take advantage of economies of density, in order to provide the most efficient modal choice to serve the needs of shippers or consignees. Box 4.1 highlights the experience of Zaragoza and the critical role of government.

INVESTING IN DETAILED ANALYSIS OF DISAGGREGATED NATIONAL FREIGHT FLOWS

Conventional commercial and marketing strategy and planning for rail organizations usually consists of strategies for internal organization or improvements in operational efficiency. The outcomes are related to identifying how to reduce the price of rail as a mode, with the aim of improving customer willingness to pay. The challenge with using this type of strategy is how to strategically position freight rail within a national logistics context.

Most emerging economies do not have the advantage of several decades of gradual development of national or regional logistics. Policy makers may therefore have limited information on commodity volumes, freight types, transport supply, origins and destinations, and key participants in supply chains. If such information does exist, it is often incomplete or partial. In most countries, for example, data on road traffic counts may be available, but they may not be related to industry productivity data, warehousing data, or rail data, and vice versa. Making informed policy decisions about where to target interventions or public investments to ensure that the right freight flows on the right mode and creates enablers to maximize the efficient use of the entire transport and logistics network is therefore challenging.

The advantage for most emerging economies is that the critical transport and logistics network is still to be built. A comprehensive national freight flow model with integrated data will support decision making in areas such as the following:

- *Colocating.* Warehousing and logistics clusters have to be optimally located. Knowing the nature of the supply chain and understanding the flow of freight can point the way to colocation of primary and intermediate suppliers and ancillary services.
- *Bundling cargo.* Data can help inform where to develop logistics hubs suited for consolidating freight for multimodal solutions that involve rail and waterways. Transport patterns will reveal opportunities for optimizing different modes and shifting freight that should naturally be on rail and waterways.

- *Creating more efficient networks in the private and public spheres.* Understanding detailed freight flows is crucial for designing distribution and storage networks for e-commerce, high-value manufacturing, and fast-moving consumer goods. The public sector can better align complementary investments such as urban transport, housing, and social services.
- *Boosting the growth of micro, small, and medium-size enterprises.* Freight data can reveal the best areas in which to locate incubators and the points of freight agglomeration that allow smaller businesses to ship at competitive rates.

A well-known barrier for shippers moving to rail and multimodal transport is the lack of critical mass, which leads to the choice of road transport. Networks of neutral logistics advisors are a proven instrument to support the bundling of freight flows of individual shippers to lower these barriers. They promote horizontal integration of and cooperation between shippers on a neutral basis, not in a role as forwarder or third-party logistics provider.

USING TAXES, SUBSIDIES, AND INCENTIVES TO CREATE MOMENTUM FOR MULTIMODAL TRANSPORT

Taxes, tax relief, and subsidies have been used with varying degrees of success. These direct and indirect interventions ultimately affect the price paid by users and can therefore influence the attractiveness of one transport mode or route over another. Customs exemption for goods transported on certain modes encourage the use of such modes; indirect taxes increase the variable cost of providing a service. Alternatively, grants can be provided to companies that move freight by modes other than road. Subsidies can be effective where there are large upfront, or fixed, costs. Because the decision of how to structure fiscal measures can affect behavior, and therefore the desired outcomes, a general requirement should be to assess the impact and effectiveness of fiscal measures before implementing them (box 4.2).

BOX 4.2

Using grants and incentives to promote intermodal rail–road transport and modal shift in Germany and the United Kingdom

Germany promotes intermodal transport in various ways. A federal program provides up to 80 percent of the eligible investment costs for the construction of new intermodal terminals (rail–road or water–road) by nonstate-owned organizations. Trucks performing pre- and post-haulage to and from intermodal terminals are exempted from the vehicle tax and are allowed to have a gross weight of 44 tons (instead of 40 tons) resulting in a shift of heavy trailers or containers from road to rail.

In the United Kingdom, following an assessment of rail freight growth potential and a review of constraints, the Department for Transport designed a rail freight strategy that uses pricing instruments to promote a modal shift from road to rail freight. Its strategy forms part of a wider set of policy objectives that aim to reduce congestion, travel times, and emissions. The intervention includes three grant schemes focused on enabling water and rail to compete with road on costs.

For companies wanting to move freight by rail and water instead of road, freight facility grants assist with the extra costs. The grants can be used to offset the capital costs of providing the required freight handling facilities or can be invested in existing facilities. A mode-shift revenue support scheme assists companies with the operating costs of moving freight by rail or inland waterway instead of road.

CHAMPIONING PILOTS THAT FOSTER COOPERATION AND CONSOLIDATION OF FREIGHT

Various actors play roles in addressing barriers and bottlenecks. Initiatives to bundle cargo can come from the logistics service providers or from shippers themselves. Facilitators, such as infrastructure managers and policy makers, can stimulate and initiate activity. For example, the European Commission initiated the Platform for Multimodality and Logistics in Inland Ports to explore interventions to address barriers to the development of multimodal transport. The main issue was how to increase the bundling of cargo flows to develop an efficient multimodal transport system that will achieve the economies of scale needed to be competitive with direct road haulage. The platform identified numerous good practices and promising concepts:

- Creation of a network of multimodal terminals with seamless connection between modes (for example, the extended gate concept with synchromodal options run by the European Container Terminal)
- Cooperative planning of terminal slots (for example, the Nextlogic/BREIN project in the Port of Rotterdam)
- The pooling of cargo flows of multiple shippers in Belgium and the Netherlands, supported by networks of neutral logistics advisors identifying potential for clustering flows of individual shippers
- Coordinated marketing between inland terminals
- Vertical cooperation between shippers and inland terminals (for example, Duisport, which runs the facilities at the Duisburg inland terminal and acts as a logistics service provider for the automotive and the chemical industry)
- Platforms for planning for urban freight and multimodal logistics
- The locating of clusters of European distribution centers, production plants, commercial zones, assembly points, and industrial complexes close to inland terminals
- The Port of Rotterdam Masterplan for port extension, with modal split targets for rail and barge hinterland transport included in the terminal concessions
- Application of information and communications technology systems to increase the efficiency and sustainability of infrastructure, by supplying both static and dynamic information about infrastructure conditions and traffic forecast
- Neutral booking platforms that integrate rail and inland waterways

Each of these suggestions emerged from joint efforts to find solutions among several public and private participants. With rail organizations part of these conversations, it is possible to experiment with innovations in logistics that play to the strengths of rail as a mode, thereby facilitating increased modal share.

www.ingramcontent.com/pod-product-compliance
Lightning Source LLC
Chambersburg PA
CBHW082113210326
41599CB00033B/6684